W9-BEW-802

The BARE BONES BIBLE™ BIOS

JIM GEORGE

HARVEST HOUSE PUBLISHERS

EUGENE, OREGON

Unless otherwise noted, Scripture quotations are taken from the New King James Version. Copyright ©1982 by Thomas Nelson, Inc. Used by permission. All rights reserved.

Verses marked NASB are taken from the New American Standard Bible ®, © 1960, 1962, 1963, 1968, 1971, 1972, 1973, 1975, 1977 by The Lockman Foundation. Used by permission. (www.Lockman.org)

Cover by Dugan Design Group, Bloomington, Minnesota

Cover illustration © Dugan Design Group

The Bare Bones Bible is a registered trademark of The Hawkins Children's LLC. Harvest House Publishers, Inc., is the exclusive licensee of the trademark THE BARE BONES BIBLE.

Due to the intentionally brief treatment of each Bible character as presented in this handbook, disputed dates, themes, or authorships are not discussed. For such information, please consult more comprehensive resource works that are designed to take such various views and details into consideration.

THE BARE BONES BIBLE® BIOS
Copyright © 2008 by Jim George
Published by Harvest House Publishers
Eugene, Oregon 97402
www.harvesthousepublishers.com

Library of Congress Cataloging-in-Publication Data

George, Jim, 1943-
The Bare Bones Bible bios / Jim George.
    p. cm.
  ISBN-13: 978-0-7369-1540-3
  ISBN-10: 0-7369-1540-0
  Bible—Biography. I. Title.
  BS571.G45 2008
  220.9'2—dc22

                                                                    2007036132

All rights reserved. No part of this publication may be reproduced, stored in a retrieval system, or transmitted in any form or by any means—electronic, mechanical, digital, photocopy, recording, or any other—except for brief quotations in printed reviews, without the prior permission of the publisher.

Printed in the United States of America

    08 09 10 11 12 13 14 15 16 / LB-NI / 12 11 10 9 8 7 6 5 4 3

Contents

Welcome to the Key People of the Bible!

It is my desire that *The Bare Bones Bible Bios* become a favorite resource tool to acquaint you with the major personalities of the Bible or remind you afresh of the men and women whom God used through the centuries to fulfill His sovereign plan. The biographies in this book are arranged in the order they appear in the Bible, with one exception—Jesus Christ is presented last because He is the central focus and ultimate consummation of God's plan of salvation. I pray that these biographical sketches will stimulate you toward a lifetime of reading and studying the lives of those who were strategic in God's working in history.

The goal of these selected biographies is to give brief overviews about the lives of the key people in Bible history. Due to these intentionally short treatments, disputed dates and events are not discussed. For an in-depth study of any of these biblical personalities, please refer to more comprehensive works on their lives.

Adam
The First Man

*Then the LORD God took the man and put him
in the garden of Eden to tend and keep it.*
GENESIS 2:15

☖

Most notable quality: Innocence
Most notable accomplishment: First human
Date lived: 930 years from the beginning of recorded history (lived
930 years)
Name: *Adam*, meaning "mankind"
Major text: Genesis 2:1–5:5

Bare Bones Background

"In the beginning God created the heavens and the earth" (Genesis
1:1). These renowned words open the Bible and point to the beginning
of all creation and to Adam, our head, the beginning of all mankind. In
him all of humanity's future dwelt. In him all possess the uniqueness of
being created in the image of God. From him we learn what might have
been—sinless existence. And in Adam we also come face to face with
the effect of his sin.

Quick Sketch

Adam, first human and the first to experience God's perfection, provides a glimpse of what God originally intended for mankind—a perfect relationship with Him in a perfect environment of perfect health and perfect peace. Unfortunately, Adam, and his wife, Eve, make a decision that takes the human race down the path to sin, misery, and death.

But God does not leave Adam and Eve and mankind without hope. God promises that a descendant of the woman will someday defeat evil and especially the evil one, as represented by the serpent in the Garden of Eden. Speaking to Satan, who had used the serpent, God explains that one who is to come (Jesus Christ) "shall bruise your head," meaning a fatal blow will eventually be given to Satan (3:15).

The Big Picture

▶ Adam is created in God's own image—*Genesis 1:26-27*

"Let us make man in Our image, according to Our likeness," is God's statement about what would be His crowning act of creation. Adam would be created to enjoy a unique, personal relationship with his Creator. This relationship would clearly differentiate Adam from the rest of creation. In his rational life, Adam would be like God in the sense of possessing reason, will, intellect, and emotions. In a moral sense, Adam would resemble God in goodness and sinlessness—a perfect man. However, as a created being, Adam would also find himself susceptible to temptation.

▶ Adam is given dominion—*Genesis 1:27-28*

With Adam's creation comes responsibility and a job assignment: He is to "subdue" the Earth and "have dominion" over every living thing. The Earth is a perfect leadership laboratory for Adam. He has a perfect mind for making right decisions, a perfect environment to "tend and keep" (2:15), and best of all, a perfect "boss" who gives him plenty of room to exercise his leadership.

▶ Adam is given a helper—*Genesis 2:21-24*

Adam is incomplete without someone to complement him. Therefore God graciously gives Adam a companion—a woman, Eve—who is like him in that she comes from his flesh, from one of his ribs. They are to fulfill each other. The two of them together are to be a greater sum than their separate lives. They are to be the "perfect team."

▶ **Adam is susceptible to temptation**—*Genesis 3:1-7*

Adam is created a sinless being, but his sinlessness is yet untested. Eve, Adam's counterpart, is the first to be approached and tempted by Satan, who speaks to her through a serpent. Eve is deceived by the snake and disobeys God by eating fruit He had expressly prohibited. Next Eve asks Adam to join her in eating the same forbidden fruit. Adam does not resist Eve's offer; he eats with full knowledge his action is wrong (1 Timothy 2:14). The couple's sin is more than that of merely eating the fruit: They disobey the revealed word of God. Adam and Eve believe the lies of Satan, and put their own wills above God's will.

The Portrait

God communicated clearly to Adam: "Of every tree of the garden you may freely eat; but of the tree of the knowledge of good and evil you shall not eat" (Genesis 2:16-17). When Adam and Eve chose to eat the forbidden fruit anyway, sin entered the human race with all of its terrible consequences (Romans 5:12), including...

- shame (Genesis 3:7)

- separation from intimate fellowship with God and immediate spiritual death (verse 8)

- strife in their marriage relationship as their oneness degenerated into blaming (verse 10)

- strife in Adam's relationship with God as he chose to blame God: "The woman whom You gave to be with me, she gave me of the tree, and I ate" (verse 12)

- suffering, toil, pain, and inevitably physical death (verses 16-19)

Life Lessons from Adam

God spoke His will directly and clearly to Adam, and today God speaks to you through His Word, the Bible, with the same directness and clarity. Choose to listen as:

- *God communicates His will*—The Lord personally and clearly gave Adam one limitation: Don't eat the fruit of one specific tree. God also told Adam exactly what would happen if he did eat the fruit. Yet Adam chose to disobey God and do things his way. Today you can save yourself much grief, misery, and heartache by looking to God and doing things His way.

- *God communicates through His Word, the Bible*—Obviously God communicated with Adam differently than He does with His people now. Today God reveals His will in the Bible. In it you will discover everything you need for life and godliness (2 Peter 1:3).

- *God communicates the way to salvation*—Sin and death began in the Garden of Eden. Yet in that same garden, God gave hope that one would come to defeat the power of sin. Sin's power ended in another garden in Gethsemane thousands of years later as Christ, the one prophesied—the "last Adam" (1 Corinthians 15:45)—willingly died on a cross for sinners, releasing them from the bondage of spiritual death. "Now is the day of salvation" (2 Corinthians 6:2). If you have not yet placed your trust in Christ, do so today.

The Fall

"The fall" speaks of the moment Adam and Eve first disobeyed God. Adam and Eve fell from a righteous standing before a holy God. Their fall brought sin into every person's life (Romans 5:12). Sin is inborn, a part of our nature, and resides in us. Subsequently, every human has inherited the effects of Adam's sin (Romans 3:23).

The Grace of God...

(Genesis 3:9-24)

...sought out Adam
...promised a Savior
...clothed Adam
...removed Adam from the garden
...provided for Adam's physical needs

Eve
The First Woman

*It is not good that man should be alone; I will
make him a helper comparable to him.*
GENESIS 2:18

&

Most notable quality: Innocence
Most notable accomplishment: First woman, wife, and mother
Date lived: From the beginning of recorded history
Name: "Woman, because she was taken out of Man" (Genesis 2:23);
named *Eve* after the fall "because she was the mother of all living,"
meaning "life" or "life-giving" (3:20)
Major text: Genesis 2:1–5:5

Bare Bones Background

After Adam is created, he enjoys the blessing of fellowship and communion with God, the blessing of pure beauty in an unspoiled world, the blessing of pleasure and fulfillment in his work, and the blessing of God's provision. Yet God declares, "It is not good that man should be alone; I will make him a helper comparable to him" (Genesis 2:18).

Enter Eve.

Quick Sketch

Unlike Adam, who was created whole from the dust of the ground, Eve is created whole from a bone taken from Adam's side. The first husband and wife, Eve and Adam enjoy perfect marital bliss until Eve succumbs to temptation, eats the fruit God had forbidden, then offers it to Adam, who also eats. Sin and sorrow enter their perfect world and perfect marriage, and God drives them out of their perfect home in the Garden of Eden. The births of their first sons, Cain and Abel, brings more grief culminating in Cain murdering Abel. At last, righteous Seth is born.

The Big Picture

▶ **Eve is the first woman**—*Genesis 2:21-22*

Fashioned by God from one of Adam's ribs, Eve arrives on earth a complete, mature, grown woman, not to mention perfect.

▶ **Eve is the first wife**—*Genesis 2:18-24*

God observes that it is not good for the man Adam to be alone. Therefore He makes a helper for him—a companion and counterpart, one unlike him in that she is a woman, yet one like him, comparable to him, a human. When Adam first sees Eve, he says, "This is now bone of my bones and flesh of my flesh; she shall be called Woman, because she was taken out of Man" (verse 23). Regarding the union of a man and wife, God states, "Therefore a man shall leave his father and mother and be joined to his wife, and they shall become one flesh" (verse 24).

▶ **Eve is the first to be tempted by Satan**—*Genesis 3:1-6*

Enter the serpent. Satan uses a snake in the Garden of Eden to approach Eve and tempt her by questioning God and twisting what God had told Adam. Innocent and unsuspecting, Eve is no match for the devil. At last she succumbs and eats the fruit God had forbidden. To make matters worse, she offers the same fruit to her husband, Adam, and he too eats. As a result of Adam and Eve's sin, they are expelled from the Garden of Eden and their relationship with God and one another is altered, affecting the Earth and all mankind.

▶ **Eve is the first mother**—*Genesis 4:1-2*

God tells the serpent, the devil, that Eve's "seed" will bruise the serpent's head (3:15). This is the first mention and promise of a Redeemer,

Immanuel-Christ. One day Christ would come and provide a glorious victory over sin and Satan.

When Eve does conceive and bears her firstborn son, Cain, she may have been expecting the fulfillment of God's promised Messiah. This is not the case, as Cain is an evil man who murders his brother, Abel, a righteous man who pleases God. Because of his crime, God sends Cain away, multiplying Eve's loss and also making her the first mother to have a child die. In time yet another son, Seth, is born to Adam and Eve. It is through Seth that God will perfect His promises.

The Portrait

No woman has ever had the privilege Eve enjoyed of walking and talking with God in a perfect environment. Eve had more than any woman has ever had since—a perfect marriage, a perfect and problem-free environment, and everything she needed. And yet she wanted more. She wanted to eat of the one tree God had declared off limits. She wanted more knowledge, more power, more wisdom, to be like God. Therefore, "when the woman saw that the tree was good for food, that it was pleasant to the eyes, and a tree desirable to make one wise, she took of its fruit and ate. She also gave it to her husband with her, and he ate" (3:6). Eve saw, desired, took, ate, and gave.

Through the woman, sin and death entered the world (1 Timothy 2:13-14). But through the seed of the woman also came redemption from sin—the Messiah, the Redeemer, the Savior Jesus Christ.

Eve tasted the bitterness of personal sin and its consequences, but she also partook of God's goodness, provision, and protection as He clothed her and her husband, taught them to make garments for themselves (3:21), drove them out of the Garden of Eden, and set cherubim and a flaming sword at its entrance so they might not eat of the tree of life (3:24).

Life Lessons from Eve

Beware!—Sin is always around the corner. Temptation is a part of daily life. "Be sober, be vigilant; because your adversary the devil walks about like a roaring lion, seeking whom he may devour. Resist him, steadfast in the faith" (1 Peter 5:8-9).

Rejoice!—Marriage was designed by God and is meant to complete each partner. Like Eve, a wife is to help her husband and together live out God's will.

Believe—Never doubt God's Word, His character, or His love. Satan sought to malign God and twist His Word, but God had always taken care of Eve and Adam, and God always would. Like David, you can know and declare, "The LORD is my shepherd; I shall not want" (Psalm 23:1).

Trust—Despite the sorrows of sin, you can count on God's faithfulness and forgiveness. Rely on His promises, and have faith in His goodness.

Sentencing by God in the Garden
(Genesis 3:14-19)

To the serpent: "Because you have done this, you are cursed more than all cattle, and more than every beast of the field; on your belly you shall go, and you shall eat dust all the days of your life. And I will put enmity between you and the woman. And between your seed and her Seed; He shall bruise your head, and you shall bruise His heel" (3:14-15).

To the woman: "I will greatly multiply your sorrow and your conception; in pain you shall bring forth children; your desire shall be for your husband, and he shall rule over you" (3:16).

To Adam: "Because you have heeded the voice of your wife, and have eaten from the tree of which I commanded you saying, 'You shall not eat of it': Cursed is the ground for your sake; in toil you shall eat of it all the days of your life. Both thorns and thistles it shall bring forth for you, and you shall eat the herb of the field. In the sweat of your face you shall eat bread till you return to the ground, for out of it you were taken; for dust you are, and to dust you shall return" (3:17-19).

Cain

The First Murderer

Now Adam knew Eve his wife,
and she conceived and bore Cain, and said,
"I have acquired a man from the LORD."
GENESIS 4:1

☘

Most notable quality: Representative of evil
Most notable accomplishment: First murderer
Date lived: At the beginning of recorded time
Name: *Cain*, meaning "to acquire" or "to get"
Major text: Genesis 4:1-17

Bare Bones Background

Two brothers, Cain and Abel, usher in the world's first "second generation." Adam and Eve had been driven from the Garden of Eden as an act of mercy on God's part (Genesis 4:22-24). Beyond the borders of their former perfect home, Adam and Eve seek to obey God's command to "be fruitful and multiply" (1:28). This seems implied by Eve's comment when she gives birth to Cain, the first baby ever born—"I have acquired a man from the LORD" (4:1). Some time later, Abel is added to this first family.

Quick Sketch

In Cain, Eve may have thought God was giving her the promised

Savior referred to in Genesis 3:15. (Oh, how harshly she will learn this not to be so!) But before Eve has much time to think about the birth of her firstborn, Cain, she has a second son, Abel.

The Big Picture

▶ **Cain's occupation and offering**—*Genesis 4:2-4*

Cain is a tiller of the ground, a farmer. When he and his brother bring special gifts to Jehovah to express their gratitude to Him in conjunction with their worship (the first recorded account of an act of worship), Cain offers the fruit of his crops. His brother, however, a keeper of sheep, brings an offering of the firstborn of his flock.

▶ **God's response to Cain's offering**—*Genesis 4:3-5*

After the two brothers present their individual offerings, God approves of Abel and his offering, but "did not respect Cain and his offering" (verse 5). Hebrews 11:4 indicates Cain lacked faith, and God had seen what was and was not in Cain's heart.

▶ **Cain's response**—*Genesis 4:5*

After having his offering rejected by God, Cain has a choice to make regarding his response. He could either repent of his sin and lack of faith and reverence toward God and choose to approach Him with a right attitude of heart, or he could become hostile toward God. Unfortunately, Cain chooses the latter option and adds yet more sins to a growing list of offences—jealousy and unbridled anger toward his righteous brother.

▶ **God's solution**—*Genesis 4:6-7*

Gently and patiently, God seeks to deal with the rebellious Cain. He reminds this erring man of what he needs to do: "If you do well, will you not be accepted?" God also warns Cain that "sin lies at the door. And its desire is for you." Carefully God cautions Cain to repent quickly before sin, like a crouching beast, springs up and consumes him. The Lord explains that sin can be resisted, telling Cain, "You should rule over it."

▶ **Cain's solution**—*Genesis 4:8*

Cain is at a crossroad. His next decision can put him on a path of forgiveness, reconciliation, joy, and usefulness to God, or on a track of defeat and separation. Cain rejects the wisdom spoken to him by Jehovah to do the right thing. He refuses to repent and, just as God had cautioned, the sin of jealousy that lay at Cain's door rises up and, like a lion, consumes him and turns him into the world's first killer: "Cain rose up against Abel his brother and killed him."

▶ **Cain's curse**—*Genesis 4:9-17*

God curses Cain and banishes him to a desert that does not produce crops and food. For as long as Cain lives, he will wander from one dry wasteland to another in search of sustenance. He will be removed from the circle of God's care. However, God, in a final act of mercy, "set a mark on Cain, lest anyone finding him should kill him" (verse 15).

The Portrait

Cain and his relationships with God and his brother is a remarkable study because it demonstrates the age-old, ongoing struggle between right and wrong, good and evil. There are two ways of living—God's way, and man's way. And there are two destinies that result from a person's choices and lifestyle—acceptance or rejection by God.

Obviously, Cain is an example of evil. He is named in the New Testament as representative of those who do not possess the new birth in Christ and are the children of the devil. They are lovers of evil and children of the wicked one (1 John 3:12). They do not practice righteousness, and they do not love others. Cain did not love God nor his brother.

Life Lessons from Cain

Cain's evil actions shout across the generations with a list of warnings and instructions:

- When you worship God, a correct attitude is mandatory.
- The opportunity to do what is right is available at all times.

- Sin is always lurking nearby, at your doorstep, but it can be mastered.

- Uncontrolled anger will lead to sin.

- Anger accompanied by evil actions never achieves God's righteous plan.

- There are always consequences to wrong choices.

That which is in your heart will eventually come out in your actions. Jesus said, "A good man out of the good treasure of his heart brings forth good things, and an evil man out of the evil treasure brings forth evil things" (Matthew 12:35). Ask God often to search your heart for any sin or wickedness (Psalm 139:23).

The Romans Road
The Road Leading to Christ

—"All have sinned and fall short of the glory of God" (Romans 3:23).

—"The wages of sin is death, but the gift of God is eternal life in Christ Jesus our Lord" (Romans 6:23)

—"God demonstrates His own love toward us, in that while we were still sinners, Christ died for us" (Romans 5:8).

—"If you confess with your mouth the Lord Jesus and believe in your heart that God has raised Him from the dead, you will be saved. For with the heart one believes unto righteousness, and with the mouth confession is made unto salvation" (Romans 10:9-10).

Abel

The First Martyr

*Now Adam knew Eve his wife,
and she conceived and bore Cain...
Then she bore again, this time his brother Abel.*
GENESIS 4:1-2

☘

Most notable quality: Representative of good
Most notable accomplishment: A heart for God
Date lived: At the beginning of recorded time
Name: *Abel*, meaning "breath, a fleeting breath, a vapor"
Major text: Genesis 4:1-17

Bare Bones Background

Abel is one of the two initial sons born to Adam and Eve. His older brother is Cain, a representative of evil. The Bible gives no time interval between Cain's birth in Genesis 4:1 and Abel's in verse 2. All we know is they are two brothers with two different occupations, two varying hearts, and two diametrical dispositions. No wonder their lives turn out so differently!

Quick Sketch

Can you imagine attempting to raise an evil son and the heart-ache such a child would induce? Adam and Eve's firstborn, Cain, is not only evil, but so vile that he comes to stand for all the children of the devil, for all who are lovers of evil and children of the wicked one (1 John 3:12). But then another child is born, one who comes to be known as "righteous" Abel (Hebrews 11:4). Joy at last enters Adam and Eve's daily life. But even greater grief is to come: Cain kills Abel. What happened?

The Big Picture

▶ **Abel's occupation and offering**—*Genesis 4:2-4*

Abel is a keeper of sheep. He is the originator of pastoral life, while Cain follows in his father's footsteps and pursues agriculture. Nothing in Scripture suggests that either the keeping of sheep or being a tiller of the ground is to be more respectable than the other occupation. In fact, most people in Bible times subsisted on a combination of both.

The difference between the two brothers becomes evident when each brings an offering to the Lord. Cain's offering to God is produce "of the fruit of the ground." But Abel's offering is "the firstborn of his flock and of their fat," the very best he could bring.

▶ **God's response to Abel's offering**—*Genesis 4:4-5*

Man looks at the outward appearance, "but the LORD looks at the heart" (1 Samuel 16:7). When God looks at the hearts of these two brothers, He "respected Abel and his offering, but He did not respect Cain and his offering." The writer of Hebrews explains: "By faith Abel offered to God a more excellent sacrifice than Cain, through which he obtained witness that he was righteous, God testifying of his gifts; and through it he being dead still speaks" (11:4). Abel, with his offering, approaches a holy God with the right attitude for worship.

▶ **Abel's death**—*Genesis 4:5-8*

Abel becomes the world's first martyr while Cain becomes the world's first murderer. Cain is furious over God's rejection of him and his offering. He is also extremely angry about God's approval and acceptance of Abel and his offering. The result? Cain's wrath boils over and he "rose up against Abel his brother and killed him."

The Portrait

Good and evil. Right and wrong. In Abel and his brother we witness the battle between these two opposing qualities. Righteousness costs, and it cost Abel his life. Yet Abel was the standard-bearer for good. He was one of the very few people in the Bible who had nothing negative said of them. In fact, Jesus named Abel as a representative figure of those who, through history, have been killed for their righteous behavior (Matthew 23:35).

Life Lessons from Abel

God said to Cain, "The voice of your brother's blood cries out to Me from the ground" (Genesis 4:10). The writer of Hebrews noted of Cain that "he being dead still speaks" (Hebrews 11:4). Abel was deemed righteous by God, therefore his messages cry out and continue to speak to us today. Hear them well:

- Always give God your best.
- Realize that the innocent will suffer unjustly.
- Set your heart on pleasing God, regardless of the cost.
- Understand that evil is a part of our world—this includes hatred, jealousy, strife, and even murder and death.

As with Cain, what's in your heart will eventually come out in your actions. For Abel, a righteous heart produced a reverence and obedience to God's commands. His faith provides an example for you to follow.

The Road to the Cross

One firstborn lamb...
> offered for a **man**, Abel (Genesis 4:4).

One firstborn Passover lamb...
> offered for a **household**, Israelite slaves (Exodus 12).

One firstborn lamb on the Day of Atonement...
> offered for a **nation**, Israel (Leviticus 16).

One Lamb of God...
> offered for a **world** of sinners, including you and me (John 1:29).

Noah

The Man Who Built the Ark

Noah found grace in the eyes of the LORD.
GENESIS 6:8

&

Most notable quality: Perfect in his generation
Most notable accomplishment: Built an ark
Date lived: Before, during, and after the Flood (lived 950 years)
Name: *Noah*, meaning "to comfort" or "to rest"
Major text: Genesis 6–9

Bare Bones Background

As we approach the biography of the man Noah, the Bible reports nine generations have passed since God created Adam and Eve. Mankind has grown so evil that God has determined to destroy the human race (Genesis 6:13). But in the midst of rampant sin, violence, and corruption, God notices an exception in the life of one man: "Noah found grace in the eyes of the LORD" (6:8).

Quick Sketch

In the life story of Noah, we come face to face with the moral character God was looking for thousands of years ago: Noah was righteous and "a just man" (6:9), and he was obedient in all that God asked of him (6:22).

The Big Picture

▶ **God's command**—*Genesis 6:13-21*

Just as God observes the depravity of mankind in general, He also takes note of righteousness in one individual, Noah. God chooses to explain in great detail to godly Noah what He is about to do and the part Noah will play in fulfilling His desires and His plan. Noah's contribution will be a massive undertaking—build a boat 450 feet long, 75 feet wide, and 45 feet high, then fill it with representatives of every species of life on Earth!

▶ **Noah's obedience**—*Genesis 6:22–7:5*

Noah's response to his new responsibilities is immediate. With no excuses, no better ideas, no complaining, no questions asked, Noah goes right to work building the world's first-ever boat and gathering up the animals and food to feed them for a year. The biblical account says on two separate occasions—first when Noah was given the initial news of God's intentions and his part in them, and then 120 years later—"Noah did according to all that God [the LORD] had commanded him" (Genesis 6:22; 7:5).

▶ **Noah's significance in Scripture**—*Genesis 7:6–8:22*

Noah demonstrates faithfulness and obedience as he patiently preaches a warning to friends and neighbors while building a giant boat—an ark—for 120 years (6:3). In a sense, Noah becomes the second father of the human race. The New Testament cites Noah as an illustration of God's patience and grace—God waited 120 years before He brought about worldwide destruction through the Flood. When the 120 years is up, God spares righteous Noah and his family—eight souls total—and destroys an unrighteous world (2 Peter 2:5).

The Flood is universal, covering the whole earth. All that breathes air is destroyed except for whatever life is aboard the ark. The floodwaters last for over a year, then at last the land is dry again. Noah again shows his reverence and obedience to God by offering sacrifices to Him. God is pleased with Noah's sacrifices and makes a significant covenant or agreement with Noah and all mankind (Genesis 9:8-17), promising, "I will never again curse the ground for man's sake...nor will I again destroy every living thing as I have done" (8:21).

The Portrait

Against the black backdrop of evil, Noah stood out brilliantly as the only godly person on the face of the Earth. The Bible gives this threefold description of Noah's character (Genesis 6:9):

- He was a just man—Noah lived by God's righteous standards.

- He was perfect in his generation—Though not sinless, Noah's life mirrored the image of God and burned bright in comparison to the faint glow of God's morality as seen in the evil men around him.

- He walked with God—Only one other human being was given this commendation. That man was Enoch, Noah's great-grandfather (5:24).

Life Lessons from Noah

Noah's relationship with God was reflected in his influence on his world. Noah was totally sold out to God; therefore, he was qualified to be God's instrument of salvation and judgment. It didn't matter to Noah what others thought of him before God asked him to fashion an ark or during the 120 years it took him to build it. Noah found grace in the eyes of the Lord (Genesis 6:8) and was a pleasure to the Lord. What can you learn from Noah's life and character?

- *Noah was obedient to do what God asked*—Whether it was the massive undertaking of creating a never-before-boat or the work of gathering up animals, Noah carried it out.

- *Noah was obedient to the letter of God's instructions*—The Lord gave Noah specific instructions for building the ark (the kind of wood to use, the exact measurements, the number of stories and windows). He was also specific about Noah gathering "two of every sort into the ark...male and female" (verse 19). Whatever God asked, Noah did it God's way.

- *Noah believed and trusted in God*—"By faith Noah, being divinely warned of God of things not yet seen, moved with godly fear, prepared an ark for the saving of his household; by the which he condemned the world, and became heir of the righteousness which is according to faith" (Hebrews 11:7).

Noah was a reflection of God and that was all God needed to work powerfully through him. The same holds true today: God is still looking for righteous and obedient men and women. If God sees such qualities in you, He can use you powerfully in extraordinary ways to transform your family, your work, your church, even your world. Make whatever changes you must to ensure you are living for God. By faith, do whatever it takes to follow God completely.

What witness did God give mankind before the Flood?
- His creative handiwork—Romans 1:20
- His law in man's heart—Romans 2:14-15
- A conscience—Romans 2:15
- The knowledge of sacrifice—Genesis 4:4
- The preaching of Enoch—Jude 1:14-15
- The Spirit of God—Genesis 6:3
- The preaching of Noah—2 Peter 2:5

The Noahic Covenant
(Genesis 9:16)

It was made by God.
It was made unconditional.
It was made to all humanity.
It was made for all times.
It came with a sign—a rainbow.

Abraham

Father of the Jewish Nation

And [Abraham] believed in the LORD,
and He accounted it to him for righteousness.
GENESIS 15:6

Most notable quality: Faith and prayer
Most notable accomplishment: Father of the Hebrew race and all people of faith throughout time
Date lived: About 2100 B.C. (lived 175 years)
Name: *Abram*, meaning "exalted father," later changed by God to *Abraham*, meaning "father of a multitude"
Major text: Genesis 11:26–23:20

Bare Bones Background

At this point in God's history we are introduced to Abram, later renamed Abraham by God. Abraham is one of the most important men in the Old Testament. He first appears in Genesis 11:26 as a decendant from the line of Shem (a son of Noah), living in Ur, a wealthy and sophisticated city in the ancient region called Mesopotamia.

Quick Sketch

Nearly 100 times in the Bible God is referred to as the "God of Abraham," or Abraham is referred to as the "father" of the Hebrew people. Each notation is in reference to the man Abraham, with whom God made covenant promises. These promises are issued regardless of Abraham's often erratic behavior. With each mention we are reminded of God's grace toward Abraham.

Abraham's place in history is not merited because of his descendants, though both the Jews and Arabs claim him as their father. Nor does Abraham's honor come from his faltering attempts at being an ideal husband and father. He is highly regarded because of God's call and covenant with him and for his maturing faith, which gave him the courage to be obedient to God even under the most difficult of challenges.

The Big Picture

▶ **Early steps of faith**—*Genesis 12–15*

The patriarch Abraham's initial obedience to God's call to leave his kinsmen and, along with Sarah, his wife, follow Him (12:1-9) is rewarded with further blessing as God continues to unveil His plans for Abraham. Abraham reveals that faith does not spring up as full-blown trust in God. His first steps of faith are faltering, as he decides on his own to go to Egypt in search of food during a famine (12:10-20). But God, in His grace, continues to lead and mature His wavering servant, as we see in these events:

- God separates Abraham and his nephew Lot (13:1-18).
- God enables Abraham to rescue Lot from war lords (14:1-17).
- God further confirms the covenant with Abraham (15:1-21).
- God waits 25 years before fulfilling His promise to give a son to Abraham and Sarah.

▶ **Obstacles to a maturing faith**—*Genesis 16–24*

In these chapters we begin to witness Abraham's growth in his walk of faith. We also see that faith in God is no guarantee of a trial-free life. With Abraham's trials came more opportunities for him to exercise his faith, in such instances as:

- The scheming of Sarah to obtain a son (16:1-16)
- Trusting God's promise of a son by Sarah (17:1-27)
- Interceding with God for the lives of the righteous in Sodom (18:16-33)
- The long-awaited arrival of the promised son, Isaac (21:1-7)
- Sending away Hagar and Ishmael, Abraham's son by Hagar, Sarah's maidservant (21:8-21)
- God's challenging command that Abraham offer his son Isaac as a sacrifice (22:1-19)
- Dealing with Sarah's death (23:1-20)

The Portrait

Saving faith is an instantaneous event. At a point in time we become a "new creation" in Christ (2 Corinthians 5:17). We are born again. And just as growth follows physical birth, so spiritual growth follows spiritual birth. This means our faith—our trust in God—is a maturing process.

This was certainly the case with Abraham. His initial obedience in leaving his country and kin and going to an unknown place was followed by impatience as he quickly left the area of God's direction and His provision and went to Egypt in search of food. Later Abraham had another lapse in his maturity as he listened to others, specifically his wife. He took matters into his own hands and failed to trust in God's promise to provide a son. Ultimately Abraham's faith did withstand the challenges of everyday life, and eventually he grew strong in his trust of God even to the point of a willingness to give up his son Isaac. The writer of Hebrews describes Abraham's ultimate test of faith this way:

> By faith Abraham, when he was tested, offered up Isaac, and he who had received the promises offered up his only begotten son, of whom it was said, "In Isaac your seed shall be called," concluding that God was able to raise him up, even from the dead (Hebrews 11:17-19).

Life Lessons from Abraham

Abraham had to learn, on his own, how to live out his faith. Today you have Abraham as your model; he can serve as your guide and example. The messages of Abraham's life are wonderfully encouraging:

- Even though at times your actions are sinful or at best foolish, God knows your heart and won't give up on you.

- Your faith in God may falter at times, but as the years go by and you witness more of God's goodness and grace, your trust in Him will grow.

- Your faith in God is no guarantee of a stress-free life. In fact, God may ask you to experience greater trials than others.

- Your maturing faith will equip you for the more difficult challenges that life brings your way.

- As Abraham learned firsthand, God always keeps His promises.

- Don't take matters into your own hands. Seek God's will before striking out on your own. When God has revealed His will, follow Him and do it.

Other Key People in Abraham's Life

Lot—Abraham's nephew, who left Ur with Abraham and Sarah (Genesis 11:31; 12:4-5)

Melchizedek—King of Salem, "priest of God Most High," who blessed Abraham and to whom Abraham gave a tithe (Genesis 14:19; Hebrews 7:1-2)

Eliezer—Abraham's faithful servant who was sent to find a bride for Isaac (Genesis 24)

Keturah—wife of Abraham after Sarah died (Genesis 25:1), by whom he had six children

Sarah
Mother of the Jewish Nation

*By faith Sarah herself also received strength
to conceive...and she bore a child when
she was past the age, because she judged
Him faithful who had promised.*
HEBREWS 11:11

⚭

Most notable quality: Faithful wife to Abraham
Most notable accomplishment: Mother of the patriarch Isaac
Date lived: Approximately 2100 B.C. (lived 127 years)
Name: *Sarai*, meaning "a princess," later changed by God to *Sarah*,
meaning "princess"
Major text: Genesis 11:27–21:12

Bare Bones Background

Sarah and her husband, Abraham, are alive approximately 700 years
before Moses. She and Abraham share a common parentage, for Sarah
is not only Abraham's wife, but also his half-sister by his father Terah
(Genesis 20:12). Sarah is also the mother of Isaac, and thus the ancestress
of the Jewish nation, "a mother of nations" (17:16).

Quick Sketch

The patriarch Abraham and his wife Sarah live in the prosperous and populated city of Ur in the lush fertile region of the Euphrates River valley. Yet God asks Abraham to leave his home and kin and travel hundreds of miles to an undisclosed promised land. Sarah follows her husband to a place where they will live and die as nomads, never having a place they could call home.

Originally named *Sarai*—"a princess"—Sarah is an integral part of God's plan of redemption. Therefore, when God reaffirms His covenant with Abraham and changes Abraham's name, He also changes Sarai's name to *Sarah,* meaning "princess," reflecting her significance in His scheme for her to become the mother of the great nation of Israel. God promised that He would "bless her, and [that] she shall be a mother of nations; kings of peoples shall be from her" (Genesis 17:16).

The Big Picture

The Bible is a very concise and straightforward historical account of God's working in history. Sarah, along with her husband, account for a large segment of the history of the book of Genesis (11:27–25:10) which makes their importance obvious. Sarah, like Abraham, has a substantial role in the fulfillment of God's covenant promise by being the one to bear Abraham's heir.

Three major events in Sarah's life endanger the fulfillment of God's covenant promise.

▸ Sarah is mistaken for a single woman—*Genesis 11:29–12:9; 20:1-18*

Twice, Sarah is instructed by her husband Abraham to lie about their marriage and say she is his sister. In the first instance, when Abraham arrives in the land to where God directs him, he is immediately faced with a famine. He determines to travel south into Egypt to find food. Fearful that the Egyptians will kill him in order to take his beautiful wife, Sarah, Abraham asks Sarah to say she is his sister, which is a half-truth. Sure enough, the Pharaoh takes the exquisite Sarah into his harem, prompting God to miraculously intervene to safeguard Sarah (Genesis 12:10-19; 20:1-18). Twenty-five years later, after his disgraceful behavior in Egypt, Abraham again lies about his relationship with his wife. This time he and Sarah are in a place called Gerar, whose king is Abimelech. As in Egypt, God intervenes to miraculously protect Sarah (20:1-18).

▶ **Sarah takes matters into her own hands**—*Genesis 16:1-16*

As the years progress, Sarah becomes increasingly concerned about her childless state. After all, God had promised to make Abraham "a great nation" (12:2). She decides that, if she could not produce a successor, Abraham could take her handmaid, Hagar, as a wife in order to produce an heir. Sarah's worldly method of manipulating God's plan backfires, and Abraham, Hagar, and Ishmael, Hagar's son by Abraham, suffer because of her interference. God will most definitely fulfill His promise, and Abraham will have a child by Sarah—but not for another 16 years (21:5).

▶ **Sarah laughs in disbelief**—*Genesis 18:10-15*

In a dramatic personal appearance, God announces to Abraham, for a second time, the birth of a son to Sarah. Sarah overhears the conversation between God and Abraham, and laughs in disbelief. God rebukes Sarah for her lack of faith, reminding her who He is with His question, "Is anything too hard for the LORD?" (18:14).

Up until this encounter, God has talked with Abraham only. But now, with Sarah's inward laughter of disbelief and God's obvious knowledge of her thoughts, God confronts Sarah with her failure to trust God's ability in the midst of her inability. After years of trying to work out God's plan herself, Sarah at last understands. So when her son is born, she declares, "God has made me laugh" (21:6). This time her laugh was one of joy and delight, not skepticism.

The Portrait

Sarah, like her husband Abraham, exhibited great faith in God (Hebrews 11:11). She willingly traveled hundreds of miles into an unknown land, leaving civilization and her family to live as a nomad and follow her husband as he obeyed God's call. She also patiently withstood two episodes of being mistaken as a single woman because her husband would not declare their marriage relationship due to fear for his life. In addition, Sarah endured 25 years of infertility as she waited for God's promise of a son. Sarah's trust in God, like that of her husband's, grew slowly. But Sarah's trust did mature, and her barrenness did end with the birth of a son, Isaac.

Also, Sarah's attitude toward her husband and her chaste conduct over more than 60 years of marriage are so impressive that she is mentioned in the New Testament as a model for all wives (1 Peter 3:1-6).

Life Lessons from Sarah

Sarah's travels with Abraham and her many opportunities to trust in God provide rich lessons for believers today.

- *God's promises are fulfilled according to His timetable*—Resist the urge to rush ahead of God. Wait for Him to act on your behalf. He always keeps His promises.

- *No problem is too big for God*—What you may think to be a hopeless situation is in fact an opportunity to trust God. Instead of looking at the size of your problem, look at the size of your God.

- *The answers to God's promises often come in mysterious ways*—Don't try to guess how God will work in your life. Instead, trust Him as a faithful Father who very often works out His plan in ways you will never understand.

How to Triumph in Tough Times

Pray—"The righteous cry out and the LORD hears, and delivers them out of all their troubles" (Psalm 34:17).

Trust—"Trust in the LORD with all your heart, and lean not on your own understanding" (Proverbs 3:5).

Believe—"Faith is the substance of things hoped for, the evidence of things not seen" (Hebrews 11:1).

Wait—"I waited patiently for the LORD; and He inclined to me, and heard my cry" (Psalm 40:1).

Isaac

The Peacemaker

Then God said [to Abraham]...Sarah your wife shall bear you a son, and you shall call his name Isaac; I will establish My covenant with him for an everlasting covenant, and with his descendants after him.
GENESIS 17:19

Most notable quality: Quiet spirit
Most notable accomplishment: Passing God's covenant on to his son, Jacob
Date lived: 2005 B.C. (lived 180 years)
Name: *Isaac*, meaning "He laughs"
Major text: Genesis 21–27

Bare Bones Background

Another generation is about to be ushered in with the miraculous birth of Isaac. God had promised Abraham and Sarah a son. Finally, after 25 years of waiting, a son is born. As instructed by God, the proud parents name their son Isaac, meaning "he laughs," which is appropriate considering Abraham's reaction of laughter himself when told earlier by God that his wife, who was 90 years old, would bear him a son (Genesis 17:17).

Quick Sketch

Isaac is significant in that he is a transitional figure. He inherits God's pledge to Abraham, his father, to "make you a great nation" (12:2). This promise is now being passed down to Isaac, and it will next be extended to his son. Not only is the promise passed on, but also much of Abraham's wealth. By the standards of his time, Isaac is a wealthy man.

The Big Picture

Scripture portrays Isaac as a passive man who takes no bold actions, but is content to live in the Promised Land, in tents, leading his flocks and herds to pastures and on occasion planting and harvesting grain.

▶ Isaac's betrothal to Rebekah—*Genesis 24*

After Isaac's mother, Sarah, dies and Isaac is 39 years old, Abraham sends Eliezer, a trusted servant, on a journey to his own people in Haran to find a wife for Isaac. Abraham is concerned about the idolatry of the people living around him and desires to keep his family free from such influences and practices. The servant travels hundreds of miles to Abraham's hometown, where he meets Rebekah, Isaac's second cousin, at the town's watering well.

Rebekah identifies her family to Eliezer and takes the servant to her home, where he meets the family. The servant realizes this young woman is the answer to his prayers, quickly states his business, and asks to take Rebekah back with him to Isaac. Rebekah willingly agrees to return with the servant and became Isaac's bride.

▶ Isaac's dysfunctional family—*Genesis 25:19-28*

Isaac is 40 when he marries Rebekah, but they do not have children until he is 60 years old. During that time, Isaac prays for Rebekah to conceive. God grants his prayers, and before the twins are born, God tells Rebekah that, contrary to the custom of the day, the eldest son, Esau, will serve the younger, Jacob.

As the twins grow up, Isaac and Rebekah fall into the trap of having favorites between their sons. Isaac loves Esau for his rough and rugged outdoor hunting skills, which provides him with tasty food. Rebekah, however, loves Jacob for his mild manner and his desire to be a homebody near her. This favoritism would later lead to the permanent dissolution of Isaac's family.

▶ Isaac's time among the Philistines—*Genesis 26*

Following his father's pattern, Isaac moves his entire family and all his possessions out of the Promised Land when a famine strikes. Rather than go to Egypt, Isaac moves toward the coastal land of the Philistines. God appears to Isaac and affirms that He will continue to bless Isaac even in the land of the Philistines. In fact, God tells Isaac that his descendants will one day occupy the very land he is living in!

God blesses Isaac—so much so that the local king asks Isaac to leave because of Isaac's prosperity. As Isaac is leaving, the local king asks that a peace treaty be made between Isaac and himself.

▶ Isaac's blessing to his son, Jacob—*Genesis 27*

Isaac is old and thinks he is near death, so he summons Esau, his oldest son, and following normal customs, desires to bless him. Ignoring the word of God to Rebekah that Esau would serve the younger Jacob (25:23), forgetting that Esau had sold his birthright to Jacob (25:33), and overlooking Esau's marriage to an idolatrous foreign women (26:34-35), Isaac is still intent on giving the blessing to Esau.

But due to Rebekah and Jacob's deception and treachery, Isaac, in his blind state, gives the blessing to Jacob by mistake. Esau pleads for his father to revoke the blessing. When Isaac refuses, Esau plots to kill his brother. But Jacob is sent away to Rebekah's family before any harm could come to him. Rebekah's plotting and scheming contributes to Jacob receiving the blessing, but she pays a high price for it, dying before her favorite son returns home some 20 years later.

▶ Isaac's last years—*Genesis 37:29*

Isaac dies at age 180, living 43 additional years after pronouncing his final blessing on Jacob. Time heals the hatred of Esau toward his brother. Therefore Isaac, on his deathbed, sees his two sons together and reconciled to each other.

The Portrait

Isaac's quiet spirit was seen early on when his father, Abraham, at the command of God, took him to Mount Moriah to be offered as a sacrifice. Scripture reports no objection from Isaac even as his father raised the knife to slay him (22:1-13).

This same spirit was again seen in his refusal to be provoked when his enemies claimed his wells as their own on two separate occasions. His response was to simply move farther away and dig more wells until the dispute was over (26:18-22).

Isaac's passive spirit had its dark side as well. Like his father, Isaac asked his wife, Rebekah, to pretend they were brother and sister out of fear that he might be killed by the local Philistines, who might desire her for her beauty (26:7). The king of the Philistines happens to see Isaac caressing Rebekah, guesses they are husband and wife, and firmly confronts Isaac for his cowardice.

Life Lessons from Isaac

God constantly reaffirms His promises to His people—God's promises are unfailing. He never forgets them, but we do. Therefore God uses many avenues to remind us of His love and care. Read His Word often to be reminded again and again of His promises on your behalf.

Peace at any price is not always the right decision—The Bible speaks of the blessings of being a peacemaker (Matthew 5:9), but never at the expense of your character, your responsibilities, or God's standards. Stand up for what you believe, and trust God to protect and honor your courage.

Favoritism in a family leads to strife and division—As a parent it is much better to praise the particular qualities and abilities of each of your children rather than favor the child whose strengths or personality you appreciate most.

Manipulation may get you what you want, but not what is best—God had revealed to Rebekah that Jacob would be the one blessed over his older brother, but Rebekah faltered in trusting God to fulfill His promise in His own time and way. Therefore, Rebekah did things her way, and it cost her Jacob's presence (she never saw him again) and probably Esau's love. Learn to trust God to work in your life and circumstances in His time, in His way. You will always receive what's best.

More Facts About Isaac

Last days—the days of Isaac were 180 years, and he died and was buried alongside Abraham and Sarah and Rebekah, his wife (35:28; 49:31)

High point—trusting God when God asked his father to offer him up as a sacrifice

Low point—denying that Rebekah was his wife (26:7)

Lasting contribution—"by faith Isaac blessed Jacob and Esau concerning things to come" (Hebrews 11:20)

Additional scriptures—Romans 9:7-8; Hebrews 11:17-20; James 2:21-24

Jacob

Touched by God

Behold, I am with you and will keep you
wherever you go, and will bring you back
to this land; for I will not leave you until
I have done what I have spoken to you.
GENESIS 28:15

&

Most notable quality: Transformed nature
Most notable accomplishment: Became the father of the
Israelite nation
Date lived: Around 1950 B.C.
Name: *Jacob*, meaning "supplanter" or "grabber," renamed *Israel*,
meaning "one who has power with God"
Major text: Genesis 25–50

Bare Bones Background

Abraham, Isaac, and Jacob. These three names are strung together
multiple times in the Bible to signify the patriarchs of Israel, God's chosen
people in the line of the covenant promise that God made to Abraham
(Genesis 12:1-3). God told Abraham He would make of him "a great nation."
With the birth of Abraham's son, Isaac, God's promise began to be fulfilled.
Then Jacob was born to Isaac and Rebekah. Through Abraham, Isaac,
and Jacob, God was sovereignly forming His chosen people (Romans
9), who would one day produce the one predicted in Genesis 3:15, the
one who would defeat Satan—the Messiah, Jesus Christ.

Quick Sketch

Jacob spends his youth living as a nomad in the land of Canaan with his parents, Isaac and Rebekah, and his twin brother, Esau. But rivalry and deception involving Esau forces Jacob to flee for safety to Rebekah's family in Haran. While Jacob is away, he marries two wives and has two concubines, all of whom give him a number of children, including 12 sons. These 12 sons would go on to form the 12 tribes that make up the Jewish nation of Israel, which is named after their father, Israel.

The Big Picture

▸ Jacob trades for Esau's birthright—*Genesis 25:27-34*

In Bible times, the birthright of the eldest son was significant. When the father died, the eldest son inherited twice that of other sons and assumed the authoritative position of head of the family.

Jacob's story opens with his brother Esau returning from a hunting trip, starving for food. Jacob proposes a trade: the stew he is cooking for Esau's birthright. Esau's ready acceptance shows how little he values his favored position of eldest son. It also shows what little consideration Jacob has for his personal integrity. This trade is not binding, but it does reveal the hearts and characters of the two brothers.

▸ Jacob supplants his brother—*Genesis 27:1-40*

Years later, believing he is dying, Isaac intends to give Esau the blessing of the firstborn. But Rebekah wants the blessing for Jacob—perhaps because she remembers God's pronouncement, before the twins were born, that "the older shall serve the younger" (25:23), and perhaps because she favors Jacob over Esau. Rebekah therefore urges Jacob to pretend to be his brother. Thus Jacob deceives his now-blind father and receives Esau's intended blessing. When Isaac learns what had happened, he allows Jacob's blessing to stand and confirms the passing of the covenant promise to Jacob.

▸ Jacob meets God on the way to Haran—*Genesis 27:41–28:22*

No wonder "Esau hated Jacob" and wanted to kill him (27:41). Fearing Esau's reprisal, Rebekah asks Isaac to send Jacob back to her family. On the way to Haran, Jacob has an encounter with God. In a dream, Jacob sees angels ascending and descending on a ladder from heaven to earth. Jacob is stunned by the vision and makes a bargaining pledge to God: "If God will be with me...then the LORD shall be my God" (28:20-21). This is the beginning of Jacob's growing trust in the presence and protection of God.

▶ Jacob works for Laban—*Genesis 29:1–31:55*

Jacob providentially finds Laban, Rebekah's brother and his uncle, and agrees to work for him for seven years for the hand of his youngest daughter, Rachel, in marriage. Yet on Jacob's wedding day, Laban switches daughters, and Jacob ends up married to the elder, weak-eyed Leah.

Jacob then agrees to work for an additional seven years to marry Rachael. Leah and Rachel struggle for Jacob's love and attention and give their maids to Jacob for wives with the hope of producing more children. The end result of this domestic disaster includes 12 sons born to four different women.

During this same time, Jacob has been keeping Laban's flock and herds. God blesses Jacob's every effort by greatly increasing the herds, bringing great profit to Laban. After working for 14 years for Laban's two daughters, Jacob decides to leave Haran and agrees to Laban's terms to keep only a certain color of animal as his wages rather than take all of Laban's animals. All the others would be Laban's. With this request, Jacob puts himself entirely in the hands of God, for only God could determine which animals would be Jacob's and which would be Laban's.

▶ Jacob returns home a wealthy man—*Genesis 31–32*

By the end of six more years, God had transferred much of Laban's wealth to Jacob in spite of Laban's greed and attempts at deception. At last it is time for Jacob to return home. God reassures Jacob of His presence and directs Jacob to take his family and depart.

Even though God guarantees Jacob His protection for the trip, Jacob still fears the reprisals of his brother Esau upon his return. Hoping to appease his approaching brother, Jacob sends 550 animals ahead of his family. This is a masterful strategy, but reveals Jacob's faltering attempts to believe that God would somehow intervene.

The night before Jacob meets with his brother Esau, Jacob is involved in a unique, nightlong wrestling match with a "man" whom Jacob identifies as God in human form. Jacob refuses to release his hold on his divine opponent until the Lord blesses him. The Lord then gives Jacob a new name, *Israel,* meaning "he struggles with God."

When at last Jacob meets Esau, the two brothers embrace and weep with emotion after 21 years of troubled separation.

▶ **Jacob journeys to Egypt**—*Genesis 35–49*

After Jacob returns home and is reunited with his father, Isaac, yet another famine occurs. But earlier, God had already sent one of Jacob's sons, Joseph, to Egypt. Joseph went there as a slave, but then became a ruler elevated to second only to Pharaoh. Joseph invites Jacob and his entire family of 66 persons to come to Egypt and be spared from the devastating famine.

The Portrait

God gave His blessings to Jacob knowing full well his shortcomings of lying, deception, and manipulation. However, as Jacob was forced out of his safe environment by his own deception, he began to seek God's provision. By the end of his life, Jacob was unwilling to do anything without asking God's direction. Due to this complete transformation, God changed Jacob's name from one that meant "supplanter" or "deceiver" to one that meant "God fighter" or "he struggles with God" (Genesis 32:28).

Life Lessons from Jacob

The end never justifies the means—God told Rebekah that Jacob would receive the blessing over his brother Esau, but she failed to wait for God to intervene when it appeared Isaac would bless Esau instead. Rebekah chose to use Jacob to manipulate matters and paid a high price, never seeing either son again before her death. God never needs our help to accomplish His will.

Deception begets deception—There is always a consequence to sin. Jacob's deception made it necessary for him to flee for his life and work for many years for an equally deceptive, conniving relative. Don't count on God to bail you out of the consequences you reap when you deceive others.

Spiritual maturity is a long journey—Early in life, Jacob began relying on tricks and his own schemes to get what he wanted. At the end of his days, Jacob acknowledged God's hand in all of life and even encouraged his son Joseph to wait patiently and allow God to bring him back to the land of his fathers (Genesis 48:21). So, set aside conniving and deceit. Seek to accomplish your spiritual journey from self-reliance to God-reliance quickly and with less heartache than Jacob experienced.

Jacob's Twelve Sons

Reuben	Gad
Simeon	Asher
Levi	Issachar
Judah	Zebulun
Dan	Joseph
Naphtali	Benjamin

Joseph
Faithful and Forgiving

*As for you, you meant evil against me; but God
meant it for good, in order to bring it about
as it is this day, to save many people alive.*
GENESIS 50:20

☖

Most notable quality: Forgiveness
Most notable accomplishment: Providentially sent by God
to Egypt to save his family and the Jewish race
Date lived: 1914–1804 B.C.
Name: *Joseph*, meaning "He will add" or "may he add"
Major text: Genesis 37–50

Bare Bones Background

Joseph is the eleventh out of 12 sons of Jacob, born of Rachel, the wife whom Jacob loves most. It's no wonder, then, that Joseph is Jacob's favorite son. The land that God gave to Abraham, Isaac, and Jacob—the land of Canaan—is situated between the great powers of the north and Egypt in the south. Because it is a land bridge from north to south, Canaan has been a frequent battleground. For Abraham's descendants to thrive and develop into the great nation promised by God, they would need a safe place to thrive and live. By resettling to one of Egypt's richest agricultural areas, the new nation could multiply and form a people who would one day return to Canaan with a force large enough to drive out the nations that are living there. Joseph will play a key role in helping his father, Jacob, and the rest of his family, to resettle in Egypt during a long and severe famine.

Quick Sketch

Favoritism had destroyed the unity of Jacob's parents (Isaac and Rebekah) and his relationship with his twin brother Esau. Now prejudice would affect his own home and family as well. Jacob's favoritism of Joseph is blatant and clearly seen and felt by his brothers. Joseph's brothers resent him deeply. Intensely jealous of their teenage brother, the older brothers sell him as a slave to merchants traveling to Egypt.

Despite suffering unjustly, Joseph steadfastly trusts God, consistently makes godly choices, and ultimately is exalted to second ruler of Egypt.

The Big Picture

▶ Joseph's early years—*Genesis 37*

Joseph is one of the two sons of Rachel, Jacob's best-loved wife. Because of this relationship, Jacob shows such obvious favoritism toward Joseph that his other brothers hate him. They sell Joseph to slave merchants and then tell their father Joseph is dead. Jacob's deception of his own father, Isaac, seems to have been transmitted to his sons and right back to him in their dealings with him.

▶ Joseph in Potiphar's house—*Genesis 39*

The unjust situation in which Joseph finds himself doesn't affect his positive work ethic. After he arrives in Egypt as a slave, he soon becomes the most trusted servant of his master, Potiphar, a high official in Pharaoh's government. Potiphar puts Joseph in charge of his entire estate. Later, Potiphar's wife becomes desirous for Joseph and repeatedly makes advances to him. Joseph resists saying, "How...can I do this great wickedness, and sin against God?" (39:9). The wife of Potiphar then falsely accuses Joseph of wrongdoing, and Potiphar has Joseph put into prison.

▶ **Joseph interprets dreams**—*Genesis 39:21–41:36*

Once again Joseph's abilities and integrity lead to a promotion—this time, he becomes a prison warden's agent, helping to run the prison. While Joseph is in the prison, two high officials of Pharaoh's court end up in jail as well. Each has dreams that Joseph correctly interprets—one man would be hanged, and the other restored to his former office. Two years later, when Pharaoh has a disturbing dream and no one is able to interpret it, the formerly imprisoned official who was reinstated to office remembers Joseph's skills at interpreting dreams and suggests that he be brought before Pharaoh.

▶ **Joseph is promoted to second ruler of Egypt**—*Genesis 41*

Joseph is able to interpret Pharaoh's dreams and explains to him that seven years of plenty will be followed by seven years of severe drought and famine. Joseph then recommends that someone be put in charge of gathering enough grain to feed the nation during the seven years of famine. Pharaoh and his leaders are so impressed with Joseph that Pharaoh puts him in charge of this massive project. At age 30, Joseph is the highest-ranking official in the land, next to Pharaoh. Again, as with Potiphar and in the prison, God blesses Joseph's efforts, his trustworthiness, and his organizational skills. In Egypt, Joseph marries and has two sons, Manasseh and Ephraim (41:50-52).

▶ **Joseph is reunited with his family**—*Genesis 42–47*

After the seven years of plenty were completed, famine struck, just as Joseph predicted. The entire region is affected, but only Egypt has food. Back in Canaan, Jacob hears food is available in Egypt and sends his sons there twice to purchase grain so his family might survive. On each of their trips the brothers meet with Joseph, but do not recognize him. Finally Joseph reveals himself to his brothers, forgives them of their past actions against him, and invites his father Jacob and the entire family to settle in Egypt so he can care for and provide for them.

While in Egypt, Jacob dies. Prior to his death, he gives each of his sons a blessing. When Jacob comes to Joseph, he gives a blessing to Joseph's two sons as well, insuring that Joseph will receive a double blessing. All these years later, Joseph is still the favorite of his father.

At age 110, Joseph dies in Egypt and asks that his bones be taken back to Canaan whenever the children of Israel return there. Through a hard life and to the very end of it, Joseph trusts in God's promises for himself and for God's people. Nearly four centuries later, Moses will take Joseph's bones out of Egypt, and Joshua, Moses' replacement, will bury Joseph's remains at Shechem (Joshua 24:32).

The Portrait

Joseph played a vital role in the preservation of the Hebrew people. Even though it was a painful experience, separation from his father's favoritism and its platform for developing a prideful view of himself was used by God to develop Joseph into one of the most godly characters in the Old Testament. Joseph's resistance to temptation, his work ethic, and his integrity are beyond reproach.

As the second-most-powerful man in Egypt, Joseph selflessly dedicated himself to the well-being of his adopted land. In spite of the wrong done to him by his brothers, Joseph showed great grace in forgiving them and welcoming them to share with him God's blessings in the land of Egypt. As he explained to them, "You meant evil against me; but God meant it for good, in order to bring it about as it is this day, to save many people alive" (Genesis 50:20).

Life Lessons from Joseph

Be hesitant to talk about yourself, especially if it makes you look better than others. Confidence in your God-given abilities is a desirable quality, but be careful that you don't become proud and boastful. Go about your business in quietness and humility.

Seek excellence in whatever you do. Joseph sought to do his best in everything he was asked to do, whether in high places (the house of Potiphar) or low (the dungeon). God asks you to do your best at whatever you do, wherever you are (Colossians 3:17). Each small task done well not only honors God, but trains you, like Joseph, for greater challenges and greater service.

Resist the temptation to sin. You live in a world filled with temptations. Like Joseph, you must view sin and succumbing to sin as an affront to

God. Look to God for help and keep yourself from sinning against others. In doing so you will honor God and show respect for others.

Maintain a God perspective. Whether it was the temptation of Potiphar's wife or the actions of his brothers, Joseph always trusted God's plans for his life. No matter how desperate your circumstances may seem, look beyond your present state of affairs and trust God to work out His will in your life.

Israel's Family Tree

Jacob's Wives and Their Children

Leah	Rachel	Bilhah	Zilpah
Reuben	Joseph	(Rachel's maid)	(Leah's maid)
(First born)	Benjamin	Dan	Gad
Simeon		Naphtali	Asher
Levi			
Judah			
Issachar			
Zebulun			

Moses

The Deliverer

So the LORD spoke to Moses face to face,
as a man speaks to his friend.
EXODUS 33:11

&

Most notable quality: Relationship with God
Most notable accomplishment: Delivered Israel from Egypt
Date lived: 1520–1400 B.C. (lived 120 years)
Name: *Moses*, meaning "drawn out"
Major text: Exodus–Deuteronomy

Bare Bones Background

Some 300 years have passed since the death of Joseph, one of the 12 sons of Jacob. Joseph had been a trusted leader for Pharaoh during a desperate time of famine in the land of Egypt. At Joseph's bidding, Jacob, his father, and the entire family—66 in number—moved south from Canaan and took sanctuary in Egypt.

New rulers have now come into power who know nothing of Joseph and his contributions to Egypt's welfare. Fearing the large population of Jacob's descendants and their potential power, a new Pharaoh enslaves the Hebrews. In agony the people of Israel call out to God, who sees their oppression, hears their cry of pain, and intervenes by sending a deliverer named Moses (Exodus 3:7-8).

Quick Sketch

Moses has four major roles in the course of his service to God:

- *Moses is a miracle worker*—God empowers Moses to perform miracles. Moses serves as a channel through which God's power is clearly revealed not only to a slave nation, but also to the oppressing nation, Egypt, and its leader, Pharaoh.

- *Moses is a prophet*—God speaks through Moses to reveal His desire to bless this new nation, and proclaim His judgment of Pharaoh and his people.

- *Moses is a lawgiver*—Up until the time of Moses, the people have had no moral or social standard to live by. At Mount Sinai, Moses records God's commandments and precepts, which will help guide this new nation.

- *Moses is a leader*—Upon their departure from Egypt, the people of Israel complain to Moses and constantly challenge him. Moses struggles for 40 years to lead two generations of rebellious people to the Promised Land. Only with constant prayer and God's frequent intervention is Moses able to guide the more than two million people to the very borders of their new land.

The Big Picture

One of the most important people in the Bible, Moses' significance is evident from the more than 800 verses in Scripture that refer to him. We can break down his life into three distinct phases of 40 years each:

▶ Moses' early life—*Exodus 2:1-15*

At the time of Moses' infancy, orders are given by Pharaoh to drown all male Hebrew babies to help keep down the population of the Hebrew slaves. Moses' mother, however, places him in a reed basket in the Nile River, where Moses is found by Pharaoh's daughter. In God's providence, Moses' mother is hired to nurse him for the first three years of his life, before he is taken to live permanently in Pharaoh's house. As an adopted son of the Pharaoh's daughter, Moses receives the best education Egypt has to offer.

At age 40, Moses remembers his "roots"—probably because of his mother's early influence—and intervenes in a brawl and kills an Egyptian taskmaster who was mistreating a Hebrew slave. Moses realizes his deed has become known to Pharaoh, and he flees into the desert to preserve his life.

▶ Moses as a shepherd—*Exodus 2:15-25*

In the desert of the Sinai Peninsula, Moses encounters a group of Midianite shepherds and marries the daughter of Jethro, the group's leader. Moses spends the next 40 years learning to survive as a wilderness shepherd. During this time, Moses' grand vision of helping his people fades into a distant memory as he grows more humbled by the passage of time and the harshness of the desert.

▶ Moses as a deliverer—*Exodus 3:1–Deuteronomy*

Moses' first 40 years were lived as a privileged prince of Egypt. In his pride, he thought he could deliver the people in his own strength. After four decades as a shepherd, Moses is ready for the task of being a deliverer. Also, he is now aware of his inadequacies and realizes he needs to depend on God's strength so he can lead the people of Israel during the final 40 years of his life. As God's deliverer...

- Moses confronts Pharaoh with ten plagues. The tenth plague brings the death of the firstborn in every Egyptian family. It is at this time that Pharaoh finally permits God's people to leave Egypt and their bondage (Exodus 5–13).

- Moses leads God's people through the Red Sea, where Pharaoh's pursuing army is miraculously drowned (Exodus 14–15).

- Moses receives the Ten Commandments from God on Mount Sinai (Exodus 20).

- Moses intercedes before God on behalf of the people after they build an altar and worship a golden calf instead of God (Exodus 32).

- Moses and the people build the tabernacle from a "blueprint" given to Moses by God (Exodus 27).

- Moses numbers the men to form an army to invade the Promised Land (Numbers 1–2).

- Moses intercedes again before God when the fearful people refuse to invade the new land (Numbers 13–14).

- Moses leads the nation in a barren wilderness until a new generation replaces the previous one and is ready to take and occupy the Promised Land (Numbers 15–Deuteronomy 31).

- Moses disobeys God and is not allowed to enter the new land (Numbers 20:12). He is, however, permitted to view the land from Mount Nebo before he dies and is buried by God Himself (Deuteronomy 34).

The Portrait

Moses is the only person in the Bible described as having a face-to-face relationship with God, which sets him apart from all other Old Testament individuals. God showed Moses more of Himself than He had revealed to any fallen human being up to that time. Moses' friendship with God allowed him to intercede prayerfully for the people as a priest, to perform powerful miracles before Pharaoh as God's prophet, and to lead a great multitude effectively. As God's representative, Moses communicated the Lord's great plans for a new nation's moral and social life. He was a dominant figure in the Bible and continues to be a central figure in Judaism to this day.

Life Lessons from Moses

Life has options. Moses chose God's people over the temporary glitter of Egypt. You too have options: Do you side with a corrupt culture and all its momentary pleasures, or will you embrace the eternal truths of the Bible and allow them to be your sole rule for life and living?

Never try to run ahead of God. Life decisions, even those that seem to be the most obvious or trivial, should never be attempted without God's input through prayer, study, and wise counsel. In order to have God's blessings, you must do things His way and in His timing.

God's enablement follows God's call. Moses wrongly assessed himself as inadequate for God's use. But as in the case of Moses, God will never ask you to do anything for Him without giving you all the resources you need to accomplish the task. God will only ask you to respond and to set out in faith. He will do the rest.

Sin can be forgiven, but not always its consequence. In an impulsive moment, Moses disobeyed God, and the course of his life was changed forever. You too can count on God's grace, love, and forgiveness, but also, like Moses, you may realize the consequence of your sin as something you will regret for the rest of your life. Choose to obey God, and live with no regrets.

The Family Tree of Moses

- Father was a Levite.
- Mother was a woman of faith (Hebrews 11:23).
- Sister was Miriam who intervened when Moses was drawn out of the water to ensure that Moses' mother would get to nurse and care for him. Miriam was the leader of the women of Israel.
- Brother was Aaron, Moses' spokesman and the first high priest.
- Wife was Zipporah, daughter of Jethro, a Midianite priest.

The Passover Instituted
Exodus 12:1-13

The Passover observance was instituted at the time of the Israelites' exodus from bondage in Egypt. This observance was a memorial for the time when God's angel passed over every Hebrew home upon which blood from an unblemished lamb was sprinkled on the doorposts, but struck down the firstborn of all the Egyptian families who had not placed blood on their doorposts. Each Hebrew family was given the following instructions:

- select a lamb without blemish
- slay the lamb at twilight
- sprinkle its blood on the doorposts
- roast the lamb entirely in fire
- dress in readiness to leave
- eat the meal with unleavened bread
- burn any remaining meat
- observe this memorial each year

Aaron

The First High Priest

Is not Aaron the Levite your brother? I know that
he can speak well...Now you [Moses] shall speak
to him and put the words in his mouth. And I
will be with your mouth and with his mouth.
EXODUS 4:14-15

☘

Most notable quality: Spokesman for Moses
Most notable accomplishment: First high priest
Date lived: 1500–1400 B.C.
Name: *Aaron*, meaning unknown
Major text: Exodus–Deuteronomy

Bare Bones Background

The nation of Israel leaves Egypt as a mass of two million people divided between 12 tribes, but having no unified organizational or religious structure. God initially leads the people to the base of Mount Sinai, where He will use Moses' leadership to organize the men into a fighting army and will give Moses exacting instructions concerning a central place of worship, the tabernacle, and details on regulating a set of sacrifices and feasts that are to be observed. Also, a high priest, a formal priesthood, and a group of tabernacle workers must be appointed. All of this is to be done before the troops can move on toward the Promised Land. Just as Moses was God's choice for a leader, so Moses' brother, Aaron, is God's choice for the first high priest.

Quick Sketch

Aaron is born under Egyptian slavery. His father, Amram, is from the tribe of Levi. His mother is Jochebed. Aaron has an older sister named Miriam, and a younger brother by three years, Moses. When he is 83 years old, God calls him to be Moses' spokesman to the people. Together, he and Moses withstand Pharaoh and see Israel delivered from Egypt. He is one of two men who support Moses' arms as he holds up the rod of God and gains a military victory against an army of Amalekites (Exodus 17:8-13).

When they reach Mount Sinai, God gives Moses great details as to the dress and function of the priesthood. After the construction of the tabernacle, Aaron and his sons are consecrated to their priestly offices by Moses. Aaron is God's choice to become the first high priest. Aaron stands with his brother against countless verbal attacks during the nation's 40 years of wandering in the wilderness. He shares his brother's sin at Meribah (Numbers 20:12), and along with Moses, is not allowed to enter the Promised Land. Just before Aaron dies on Mount Hor at the borders of Edom, his high priestly office is passed on to his son, Eleazar.

The Big Picture

Aaron and his sons and those who follow after him are responsible for overseeing the many and varied functions of Israel's sacrificial religious system. Because of their training and education in the law of God, they become the preeminent teachers of the people.

Aaron's role as high priest—He is to make an annual sacrifice for the people's sins on the Day of Atonement. He represents the people before God and serves as their mediator with God.

Aaron and his sons' roles as priests—They are to...

- remove all forms of uncleanliness from the people;

- determine clean and unclean animals for sacrifice;

- perform purification of women after childbirth, of people who become free from leprosy, of those who have bodily issues or secretions;

- Prohibition of relationship in marriage;

- Preside over Sabbath and annual feasts, as well as issues of land, tithes, blessings and curses, and vows.

Aaron's priestly clothing—The high priest is to wear a special outfit designed by God "for glory and for beauty" (Exodus 28:2). This outfit is unique to the office of the high priest and was to be worn by Aaron's successors.

The Portrait

Aaron was a man lost in the shadow of one of the greatest Bible characters of all times. Even though he was a co-leader in the exodus and often stood shoulder-to-shoulder with Moses against the rebellion of the people, Aaron never seemed central or essential. His greatest moments were as a follower. And tragically, two times when he did stand alone as a leader, he showed himself to be a weak man.

Aaron and the golden calf (Exodus 32)—Not long after Moses and Aaron led the people to Mount Sinai, God called Moses up the mountain to meet with Him alone. While Moses spent the next 40 days receiving the Ten Commandments and the rest of the Law under which the Israelites would live for the next 1400 years, Aaron was left in charge.

The people became nervous about Moses' long absence and demanded that Aaron make them a golden calf as a substitute for Moses' God. Aaron, without objection, complied with their wishes and even announced that the next day there would be a worship feast to God! God alerted Moses to what was happening and, when Aaron was confronted, he blamed the evil tendencies of the people and declared his version of how the golden calf appeared: "I cast [the gold] into the fire, and this calf came out" (Exodus 32:24). Aaron followed in the footsteps of many other leaders who first found out which way their people were going, then hurried to get out in front of them. Sadly, Aaron's convictions were formed by the convictions of the people.

Aaron and Miriam criticize Moses (Numbers 12)—The children of Israel left Mount Sinai after receiving the law. While they were traveling to the Promised Land, Moses' brother and sister disguised their real motive, taking over leadership, by objecting to Moses "marrying an Ethiopian woman." They asked, "Has the LORD indeed spoken only through Moses?" (Numbers 12:2). God intervened and confronted the two. Miriam was given leprosy and Aaron was strongly rebuked. Again, Aaron's weak character was exposed.

Life Lessons from Aaron

Examine yourself often for areas of weakness. Aaron was strong when he stood beside Moses, but often acted foolishly when on his own. Make an honest assessment of your strengths and weaknesses. Seek out those who can help you avoid situations you are not equipped to handle on your own. God wants you to gain the victory; often that will happen with the help of others.

Failure does not disqualify you from service. Aaron failed God and Moses on numerous occasions, yet God still used him in significant ways. You too may feel like a failure for something you have or have not done. Aaron's life can reassure you that God's mercy and grace are ready to pick you up and put you back on the path of useful service. Learn from your mistakes and ask for God's wisdom. God is ready to help if you are ready to respond to His love, forgiveness, and leadership.

Form strong convictions. Aaron was a weak leader. He wasn't willing to stand up to the people's evil request to make a golden calf. Without strong convictions Aaron caved in to the ungodly requests of the people. You are a leader on some level, whether it's as a parent or someone who desires to be a example to others. Establish your biblical convictions. Then be willing to stand for those convictions when you are asked to make a "golden calf."

Be a faithful follower. Aaron and his sister, Miriam, were envious of Moses' leadership. They wanted his position of authority, so they grumbled. God dealt with their sin. You too may desire another person's leadership position. If your motive is pride, envy, or power, then you are acting like Aaron and Miriam. The Bible tells you to obey your leaders. Obedience starts with being a faithful follower. Pray for your leaders, and ask God to show you ways to show your support for their leadership.

Aaron's Family

Brother: Moses

Sister: Miriam

Died: Mount Hor, near Edom

Honored: 30 days of mourning (same amount of time as for Moses, signifying Aaron's importance to Israel)

Sons: Nadab, Abihu—Aaron's two oldest sons, who were killed by fire

    Eleazar—took his father's place as high priest

    Ithamar—leader of the Levites, who were responsible for the tabernacle

Joshua

Conqueror of the Promised Land

[Moses] laid his hands on [Joshua] and
commissioned him, just as the LORD had spoken...
NUMBERS 27:23 (NASB)

&

Most notable quality: Loyal subordinate
Most notable accomplishment: Conquest of Canaan
Date lived: 1494–1385 B.C. (lived 110 years)
Name: *Joshua*, meaning "Yahweh is salvation"
Major texts: Exodus 17; Numbers 14; Joshua

Bare Bones Background

"Joshua fought the battle of Jericho..." So goes the chorus of an old familiar spiritual song. Who was Joshua? His life story begins in Egypt.

The children of Israel have lived and multiplied in the land of Egypt for almost 400 years. The last years of their time in Egypt are spent as slaves. Even though they are slaves, life in Egypt is considered good. Egypt is one of the most advanced civilizations of its day. But as time goes on, the Egyptian taskmasters become more cruel. So much so that the Israelites cry out to God, who then gives them Moses as their deliverer. By the force of ten plagues, Moses leads the people out of Egypt into the wastelands of the Sinai Peninsula.

One of the liberated slaves—who at the age of 50 becomes Moses' aide, his spy, his military leader, and ultimately his successor—is Joshua.

Quick Sketch

Joshua, like the rest of the Israelites, was born in Egyptian slavery. As Moses' aide and understudy for 40 years, Joshua stays by Moses' side through all the years of wilderness wandering due to the faithlessness of the people. Before Moses dies, God has Moses commission Joshua to lead the people into the Promised Land. Although Joshua is approaching 90 years of age, he is a remarkable military man and successfully conquers and settles the people in the land of Canaan, the land God had promised to their forefathers Abraham, Isaac, and Jacob.

The Big Picture

▶ **Joshua is tested early**—*Exodus 17:8-13*

After the children of Israel pass through the Red Sea when exiting Egypt, they are attacked by a band of Amalekites. Moses asks the people to choose men to defend themselves against these marauders. Joshua's military skills become evident as he successfully defeats the enemy.

▶ **Joshua is a support early**—*Exodus 24:13; 33:11*

Almost from the beginning of the exodus, when God's people flee from Egypt, Moses depends on Joshua. For example, Joshua goes part way up Mount Sinai with Moses when Moses is about to receive the Ten Commandments from God. After the tabernacle is built, Joshua is with Moses when Moses meets "face to face" with God (33:11), and stays behind as Moses reenters the camp. In these ways and others, Moses was carefully grooming Joshua to be his successor.

▶ **Joshua is trusted early**—*Numbers 14*

As the Israelites approach the land of Canaan, Moses sends out representatives from each of the 12 tribes of Israel to determine how best to invade the land. Ten of the spies return with fearful tales of giants and fortified cities, reporting "we saw the giants...and we were like grasshoppers in our own sight" (Numbers 13:33). Only Joshua and Caleb urge the people to trust God and attack as God had commanded. Because of their faith and obedience, only Joshua and Caleb are eventually allowed to enter the land.

▶ **Joshua becomes Moses' successor**—*Numbers 27:15-22*

Joshua is Moses' choice to succeed him when it becomes evident that Moses will not be allowed to enter the Promised Land. Moses had prayed for God to choose a replacement, and the Lord tells Moses publicly to appoint Joshua as his successor.

▶ **Joshua is encouraged by God**—*Joshua 1:1-9*

It was Moses' practice to have Joshua go with him whenever he met with God. In this way, Joshua was exposed to God's presence, which would strengthen Joshua's faith in the Lord for the responsibilities that were to come. After the death of Moses, God speaks directly with Joshua as the conquest of the land is about to begin:

- God promises to be with Joshua (1:2-5), to give him success (1:6), to be with him wherever he goes (1:9).

- God challenges Joshua to observe His commands (1:7-8) and not be afraid (1:9).

▶ **Joshua is a faithful leader**—*Joshua 1–24*

It takes Joshua and the people about seven years to assume control of the majority of the land. Joshua personally supervises the distribution of the land among the 12 tribes. There are still pockets of resistance in the land, and each tribe is made responsible for driving out the remaining opposition.

For the next 13 years, Joshua faithfully leads the tribes of Israel until the end of his life. When Joshua is near death at age 110, he calls the people together for one last word of exhortation. He challenges the Israelites to "choose for yourselves this day whom you will serve" (24:15). As in the past, Joshua rallies the people to renew their commitment to God. They respond, "The LORD our God we will serve, and His voice we will obey!" (24:24).

The Portrait

Joshua's leadership abilities were second only to Moses'. As Moses' influence was to the exodus, so Joshua's influence was to the conquest of the land. He was a faithful servant of Moses, and when the time came, he faithfully served God as commander of all the Israelite forces. He was committed to obeying God fully, and he was committed to insuring that the people followed God all the days of his life. The Bible's final epitaph for Joshua reads: "Israel served the LORD all the days of Joshua, and all the days of the elders who outlived Joshua" (24:31). No man could ask for better parting words than that! Not one negative is recorded in Scripture about this servant of both God and Moses.

Life Lessons from Joshua

Faithful service is essential. It is often said, "You will never learn to lead until you learn to follow." Joshua demonstrates the importance of following even in the little things. Joshua was just an aide, an errand boy, in the beginning of his service to Moses. But he was faithful and available when an important responsibility came along. Never dismiss the importance of faithfulness in the little things. Small tasks faithfully done will qualify you for the bigger tasks.

Mentoring makes a good person better. Joshua's greatness had Moses' imprint stamped upon it. Joshua bears out the fact that however great your gifts and abilities are, they can be sharpened and improved by spending time learning from someone who is more mature and experienced.

Obedience does not require comprehension. Joshua carried out the Lord's instructions at the strategic and fortified city state of Jericho—instructions that made no military sense. Nurture obedience and a readiness to trust God in spite of your lack of understanding of His ways.

Set a high standard for others. Joshua never asked his people to do or be anything he wasn't willing to do or be himself. He imposed a high standard for himself, and the people followed his example. Be sure you set a good example for your children, employer or employees, and others to follow. Never undervalue the power of your godly example to others.

Caleb, a Committed Friend to Joshua

One of 12 spies sent by Moses to survey the Promised Land

One of four men who voiced confidence to enter the land

One of only two adults who left Egypt to enter the land

One of Joshua's fearless friends, who at age 85 was still able to fight for the land

One man with great faith because he trusted in a great God

Rahab

The Harlot

*By faith the harlot Rahab did not perish
with those who did not believe, when she
had received the spies with peace.*
HEBREWS 11:31

A

Most notable quality: Shining example of faith
Most notable accomplishment: Ancestor of King David
Date lived: 1400 B.C.
Name: *Rahab*, meaning "broad"
Major texts: Joshua 2:1-21; 6:17-25; Matthew 1:5

Bare Bones Background

Poised on the plains of Moab, east of the Jordan River, Joshua and the Israelites await God's direction for conquering the land promised to them by God. In preparation for the invasion, Joshua sends two spies across the river to bring back military intelligence. They are to especially focus their attention on the great walled city of Jericho, which stood seven miles west of the river. To keep from drawing attention as outsiders while observing the city of Jericho, the two spies find their way to a place frequented by travelers and strangers—the home of Rahab, the harlot.

Quick Sketch

Rahab hides the two Israelite spies from authorities who have heard reports that the spies were seen entering her house. Having set a false trail for the authorities, Rahab asks for protection from the spies, believing that the God of the Israelites will destroy her city. She helps the spies escape by letting them down outside the city wall and warning them which road to take to avoid capture. When Jericho falls, she and her family alone of all the people of Jericho are spared. Her family is blended into the nation and she becomes a distant relative of King David, and ultimately a part of the line of the Messiah, Jesus Christ (Matthew 1:5).

The Big Picture

▶ Rahab's situation—*Joshua 2:1-3*

Three times in chapters 2 to 6, Rahab is referred to as "the harlot" or "Rahab the harlot." She is not only a heathen, but also a baseless heathen. She would have been despised in any society. As part of her profession, Rahab has a place where strangers come to lodge. These outsiders are the ones who have probably told her stories of the exodus of Israel, the parting of the Red Sea, and the overthrow of kings. So when the Israelite spies arrive on her doorstep, she has already thought through her options. It is here among strangers that the two spies hope to observe the city without being observed. Unfortunately, they are noticed going into Rahab's house.

▶ Rahab's sacrifice—*Joshua 2:4-7*

Rahab now has a choice to make. Expose the presence of the spies and be a town hero, or hide the spies and possibly face death as a traitor. Rahab believes the reports about the God of Israel and is convinced that Jericho will fall under His mighty hand. Therefore, she willfully puts her life on the line. She hides the spies, lies about their presence, and sends the authorities away on a fruitless pursuit.

▶ Rahab's scheme—*Joshua 2:8-16*

Acknowledging the fear that has gripped the people, Rahab asks that she and her family be saved when the city is destroyed. The men agree to deal kindly with Rahab when the city is taken. Their only word of caution is that their presence and mission not be exposed. Rahab helps the spies escape by letting them down with a rope from her window, which faces the outside wall of the city.

▶ Rahab's sign—*Joshua 2:17-21*

The spies tell Rahab to place a scarlet ribbon in the window from which they make their escape, and to bring her family into her house before the fighting starts. Otherwise, the spies and Israel's warriors would not be responsible for their safety. With complete trust, Rahab immediate binds the scarlet cord in the window as a sign for the invading army.

▶ Rahab's salvation—*Joshua 6:22–23*

After forty years of waiting to enter the Promised Land, the Israelite army is ready to move. The Jordan River is at flood stage, but God intervenes and parts the river so that 40,000 men could cross on dry ground. God's plan is simple: He tells the people to march around the city once each day in silence. Then on the seventh day, the people are to march around the city six times and, on the seventh round, the priests are to blow seven trumpets and the men of war are to shout, and the walls will come tumbling down. Joshua and his men do exactly as they are told and, as the walls fall, his men rush in and destroy the city completely...except for Rahab and her family, who are safe in her house.

▶ Rahab's status—*Joshua 6:25*

From this point on, Rahab's history takes a decided turn. Having faith in the God of Israel, she gives up everything associated with her country, her sinful profession, and her past. In return, she and her family are given life, a new country, and a new beginning. Rahab is taken from the very pit of sin and idiolatry and placed among the saints in the genealogy of the Savior.

The Portrait

Rahab illustrated the kind of transformation that can happen when a person puts his or her faith in God. From a human perspective, there is no reason why the Bible should speak so favorably of Rahab. She was an idolatrous heathen, a liar, a traitor who helped in the overthrow of her city, and a prostitute. You can't get much lower than that on the social ladder. Yet when you look at Rahab from the divine perspective, you see a woman with a healthy fear of God, which prompts her to welcome and hide the spies. The Bible says that this act was a visible demonstration of her faith (Hebrews 11:31; James 2:25). She becomes part of the ancestral line of Israel's greatest king, David, and ultimately the world's greatest King, Jesus Christ.

Life Lessons from Rahab

The saving power of God does not exclude even the worst sinners. Have you ever been guilty of thinking that some despicable person you know is beyond God's help? That there is just no way that person could ever be reached with the gospel? Rahab could very well have been seen in this light. Yet she, along with any other horrible sinner, is never out of the reach of God's saving arm. Don't give up on those who seem hopeless. God didn't give up on Rahab.

Faith in God transforms lives. Rahab had heard the stories of how God had parted the Red Sea and destroyed all the nations who stood in the way of Israel's path. The representatives of this God were now inside the walls of her great city. She believed in the power of Israel's God. By faith she chose to stand with Israel, even against her own people. Have you recognized God as the one true King of your life? Have you trusted in His power alone to save you? If God can transform a heathen prostitute, He can change you as well!

The salvation of others should be a concern to you. Rahab extracted a promise not only for her own salvation, but that of her family as well. There is no indication as to how close she had been to her family because of her profession, but as God began to transform Rahab's heart, she developed a concern for the salvation of her family. Do you share Rahab's heart of concern for the salvation of your family and friends? If not, maybe you have forgotten what your life was like before God saved you. Rahab didn't forget, and she didn't want her family to die without the opportunity to know the one true God.

Rahab's Place in Biblical History

Salmon and Rahab's bloodline begot Boaz

Boaz begot Obed

Obed begot Jesse

Jesse begot David

David's bloodline begot

Jesus, the Christ,

the Savior of the world

Samson

The Strongest Man on Earth

You shall conceive and bear a son [Samson].
And no razor shall come upon his head, for
the child shall be a Nazirite to God from
the womb; and he shall begin to deliver
Israel out of the hand of the Philistines.
JUDGES 13:5

Most notable quality: Faith in God (Hebrews 11:32)
Most notable accomplishment: Fought God's enemies
Date lived: Judged about 1095–1075 B.C.
Name: *Samson*, means "distinguished"
Major texts: Judges 13–16; Hebrews 11:32

Bare Bones Background

The Judges are a unique group of leaders given by God to deliver the people of Israel from the oppression of foreign powers. Israel's oppression is the result of disobedience on the part of the people. Each time Israel departs from God, He gives them over to oppressors in judgment for their sin. When the people pray for deliverance, God raises up judges to deliver them from their tormentors. This cycle occurs seven times between the conquests by Joshua until the time of Samuel. Samson, the last judge mentioned in the book of Judges, lived toward the end of this 350-year period.

Quick Sketch

Samson is born as a result of God's plan in the lives of an Israelite named Manoah and his wife. Samson's parents are given very specific instructions about how he is to be raised. He is to do a great work for God by delivering Israel out of the hand of their archenemies, the Philistines. To help Samson accomplish this assignment, God would give him supernatural physical strength. Rather than fulfill God's plan, Samson grew up to waste his strength by fulfilling his own lusts. At the end of his 20 years of judgship, Samson is tricked by Delilah, a harlot, into revealing the secret of his strength, his long hair. His secret was not actually in his hair, but in his unique relationship with God as symbolized in his pledge not to cut his hair. So Delilah has Samson's hair cut, and he loses his strength. Samson spends the last days of his life grinding grain in a Philistine prison. His final act of redemption comes as God answers his last prayer and gives him strength to pull down the pillars of a crowded pagan temple. Samson's final act for God destroys more Philistines than all those whom he killed during his life.

The Big Picture

▶ Samson's early life (Judges 13:1–14:3)

Israel again turns away from God and is suffering the consequences of their sin—God allows them to experience the oppression of the Philistines. God will provide a deliverer for Israel through a couple from the tribe of Dan. The news of this coming deliverer is brought by a very special messenger, "the Angel of the LORD" (13:3). He gives specific instruction for the mother-to-be and for the child. The child was not to drink wine, cut his hair, or touch a dead body. The child is born and as he grows, God blesses him, and the Spirit of the Lord comes upon him to help him carry out his mandate from God.

▶ Samson battles the Philistines (Judges 14–16)

Samson is supposed to lead the people in battling against the Philistines, but the fight quickly becomes personal, not political. He kills numerous Philistines, burns their fields, and is a general nuisance his entire life. His actions are done not out of concern for his people, but out of revenge for the harm the Philistines had done to him.

▶ **Samson's relationships with women (Judges 14–16)**

Samson's adult life begins with his headstrong decision to marry a Philistine girl against his parents' wishes. After she is murdered by the Philistines, Samson spends his time visiting prostitutes. His most notorious relationship is with a prostitute named Delilah, who is loyal to the Philistines. They pay her money to find out the secret of Samson's strength. When Delilah finds out the secret, she has his hair cut off and he is unable to defend himself. The Philistines capture him, blind him, and make him push a grinding wheel in a Philistine prison. What a humiliating end to a life that had such potential!

The Portrait

Samson was a man captive to his own passions and pride. He is not one you would want to emulate. However great his gifts were, his flaws were greater. His godly parents had great expectations for his life, but his strong-willed nature drove him to pursue his own pleasures rather than to protect and defend God's people. God gave him great strength to be used for God's people, but instead Samson used his abilities for his own purposes. Samson did not stay close to God, and therefore didn't live up to his potential. Although Samson judged Israel 20 years, he was never the kind of leader the earlier judges were. Samson was a great warrior himself, but he couldn't inspire others to take up the battle. Therefore, the Philistines continued to oppress Israel throughout his 20 years as judge. Yet Samson, with all his flaws and selfish motives, served God's purpose in frustrating the Philistines' plans for total domination of Israel, and he is listed among God's faithful (Hebrews 11:32).

Life Lessons from Samson

Giftedness does not equate to godliness. Samson was the most gifted man of his day. He had been given all the tools to do great things for God. Yet in his pride and stubbornness, he lived for his own passions rather than for God's purposes. Today, God has given you the stewardship of both spiritual and physical abilities. Don't squander your potential for serving God and His people. Be a wise steward and put the use of your potential in God's hands, and see how God will multiply your usefulness.

God doesn't give up on His children. Samson made a total mess of his life. He failed to achieve his potential. Yet in the end, he did look to God one last time. God answered his prayer and gave him the strength to strike a severe blow of judgment upon the leadership of the Philistines. Are you feeling guilty and separated from God because of sinful choices? God stands ready to hear and forgive and restore you to the joy of fellowship with Him. Read David's prayer of restoration (Psalm 32).

Choose to pursue God rather than flirt with temptation. Samson chose to continue in a compromising relationship with a harlot named Delilah until it cost him his sight, his freedom, and ultimately, his life. Don't see how close you can come to temptation by associating with the wrong crowd or by frequenting questionable places or doing questionable things. Rather, see how close you can stay to Jesus. Spend your time learning and growing from relationships with God's people. Follow the apostle Paul's advice to his young friend Timothy: "Flee also youthful lusts; but pursue righteousness, faith, love, peace with those who call on the Lord out of a pure heart" (2 Timothy 2:22).

List of the Judges

Judge	Tribe	Description
Othniel	Judah	Was the younger brother of Caleb
Ehud	Benjamin	Was a left-handed man
Shamgar	Unknown	Weapon of choice was an ox goad
Deborah	Ephraim	Was the only woman judge
Gideon	Manasseh	Won a military victory with only 300 men
Abimelech	Manasseh	Son of Gideon by a concubine
Tola	Issachar	Lived in the mountains
Jair	Manasseh	Father of 30 sons
Jephthah	Manasseh	Made a rash vow
Ibzan	Judah	Had 30 sons and 30 daughters
Elon	Zebulun	Judged Israel 10 years
Abdon	Ephraim	Had 40 sons and 30 grandsons

Samson	Dan	Loved Delilah and told her the secret of his strength
Samuel	Levi	Israel's greatest judge

Ruth

A Virtuous Woman

*Entreat me not to leave you, or to turn back from
following after you; for wherever you go, I will
go; and wherever you lodge, I will lodge; Your
people shall be my people, and your God, my God.*
RUTH 1:16

Most notable quality: Faithfulness
Most notable accomplishment: The great-grandmother of
King David
Date lived: During the time of the Judges (c. 1100 B.C.)
Name: *Ruth*, meaning "friendship"
Major text: Book of Ruth

Bare Bones Background

Ruth, a Moabite, appears on the scene toward the end of the period
called "the Judges" in Scripture. These are dark days, when "there was
no king in Israel; everyone did what was right in his own eyes" (Judges
21:25). Moab, a land east of the Dead Sea, is among the nations that
have oppressed Israel during this period (Judges 3:12–4:1), so there is
hostility between these two nations. A severe famine forces an Israelite
family to migrate from Bethlehem to Moab in search of food. While in
Moab the father dies, his two sons marry Moabite women, one of them
being Ruth. Then the two sons also die. Naomi, now a widow, and her
two widowed daughers-in-law must decide their future.

Quick Sketch

Ruth, a destitute Moabite widow, chooses to leave her family, country, and gods and travel back to Bethlehem with her Israelite mother-in-law, Naomi. Her sister-in-law chooses to stay in her own country and is never heard of again. With her one daughter-in-law, Naomi now makes the long trip back to Israel and her hometown of Bethlehem. Once they arrive, Naomi instructs Ruth on the customs of providing for the poor by leaving bits of grain in recently harvested fields. Ruth finds her way into the field of a man named Boaz, a relative of Naomi. Boaz has heard of Ruth's devotion to Naomi, and tells her to go to no other field, promising that he will look after her. In the end, Ruth becomes his wife, and they have a son named Obed. Obed later becomes the father of Jesse, and the grandfather of King David.

The Big Picture

Ruth is a poor widow in a desperate situation. She had married an "enemy" from outside her nation. Now her husband is dead and her mother-in-law has decided to return to Israel. Ruth has some decisions to make. Most importantly, she decided to step out in faith and form three key relationships:

Relationship #1: Ruth chooses to follow the God of Naomi. Apparently Naomi's faith motivates Ruth to know the one true God and to follow Him, even if it means leaving her country of Moab.

Relationship #2: Ruth chooses to follow her mother-in-law back to Israel rather than return to her home in Moab. There is no hesitation on her part. With resolve, Ruth voices her strong commitment to Naomi: "Wherever you go, I will go." Her declaration defies logic: Ruth and Naomi should not be close. Ruth is young; Naomi is old. Ruth is a Moabite; Naomi is an Israelite. Their countries are enemies. They have language and customs barriers. Naomi has nothing to offer Ruth except more heartache and poverty. Yet Ruth chooses to follow Naomi back to Israel and to care for her in her old age. How can this be explained? Ruth's relationship #1 decision made her relationship #2 decision easy to make!

Relationship #3: Ruth chooses to form a relationship with Boaz. Again, because of her relationship with Naomi, Ruth trusts her mother-in-law's direction for her life. Boaz, as a "relative" of Naomi's family, could act as a kinsman-redeemer. (In ancient Israel, a deceased man's relative was obligated to marry his widow and raise a son in the name of the deceased, according to Deuteronomy 25:5-10.) Ruth must perform an ancient ritual that, according to Naomi's instruction, would indicate to Boaz that Ruth desired Boaz to become her kinsman-redeemer. Boaz joyfully agrees to her proposal because she has shown herself to be a "virtuous woman" (3:11).

The Portrait

Ruth had everything going against her. She was the widow of an enemy of her country. She had no money, and she had no prospects for the future. She could have chosen to become bitter or angry at life, and angry at gods in general, including the God of her mother-in-law. But something drew her to the one true God of Naomi. There is never any indication that Ruth ever looked back after making her decision to follow Naomi and her God.

Ruth shows herself to be loyal, kind, hardworking, and trusting. Even though Ruth and Naomi face uncertain hardships, they are committed to each other and to God's care. Because each one was willing to look out for the needs of the other, they both ultimately find happiness—Ruth in remarriage and motherhood, and Naomi in her role as a doting grandmother.

Life Lessons from Ruth

Develop faithfulness even in the little things. Ruth was willing to sacrifice everything in order to faithfully assist her mother-in-law. This quality about Ruth, a foreigner, endeared her to the people of Bethlehem, and especially Boaz. Faithfulness is a fruit of the Spirit and essential if you are to live for Jesus and have a testimony to the world. How would you rate your faithfulness, even in the little things?

Be willing to submit to the guidance of others. From the first record of Ruth's life, she willingly takes the advice of her mother-in-law. She followed

Naomi's directions exactly, and never questioned her instructions. Submission is a godly response to the counsel we receive from those whom we respect and who have authority over us. God has given you the guidance of His Word, the wisdom of His teachers, and the counsel of godly peers. Listen to and heed their advice. To God, your obedience is better than any sacrifice (1 Samuel 15:22).

Allow the people of God to help in your hour of need. Ruth and Naomi returned to Naomi's hometown in a desperate condition. Yet through the aid of a family member, Boaz, their needs were met. Ultimately, Boaz married Ruth, guaranteeing her future as well. Today if you are a child of God through Jesus Christ, you have become part of His family. Allow other believers, other family members, to assist you in your hour of need. That's what family is for!

Boaz: A Virtuous Man

He was diligent (2:1)

He was friendly (2:4,8)

He was merciful (2:7)

He was godly (2:12)

He was an encourager (2:12; 3:11)

He was generous (2:15)

He was kind (2:20)

He was discreet (3:14)

He was faithful (4:1)

Hannah

A Godly Mother

*For this child I prayed, and the LORD has
granted me my petition which I asked of Him.
Therefore I also have lent him to the LORD.*
1 SAMUEL 1:27-28

&

Most notable quality: Gratitude to God
Most notable accomplishment: Gave Israel its greatest
judge
Date lived: c. 1275 B.C., during the last days of the Judges
Name: *Hannah*, meaning "gracious, graciousness," or "favor"
Major text: 1 Samuel 1:1–2:21

Bare Bones Background

Hannah is introduced to us during the last days of the Judges of Israel.
"In those days there was no king in Israel; everyone did what was right
in his own eyes" (Judges 21:25). Polygamy is a common practice of the
day, and even though Elkanah, Hannah's husband, is a godly man, he
follows this practice. Hannah is the favorite of his two wives, Peninnah
being the other. Life is hard, and survival hinges on having many sons to
help work the land, tend sheep, and carry on the family name. Therefore,
barrenness is the ultimate curse for a married woman. Unfortunately,
Hannah is barren, and has not given birth to any children.

Quick Sketch

Hannah is a beautiful example of how unpleasant circumstances can produce a beautiful outcome. Elkanah's other wife, Peninnah, torments Hannah constantly because she has no children. This harassment goes on for years. Finally grieved of heart, Hannah goes to the house of the Lord in Shiloh and vows that if God gives her a son, she will devote him to the Lord all the days of his life. God answers her prayers and she names her son Samuel, which means "asked of the Lord." After Samuel is weaned, Hannah takes her little son to the Lord's house and leaves him in the hands of Eli, the priest. Each year afterward, she brings Samuel a new robe when she comes to Shiloh to worship. Later she becomes the mother of three sons and two daughters (1 Samuel 2:21).

The Big Picture

▶ Hannah's sadness—1 Samuel 1:1-8

Hannah has been married to Elkanah for a number of years and has not borne him any children, let alone sons. In the culture of that day, barrenness was the worst thing that could befall a woman. To make matters worse, Peninnah, Elkanah's other wife, who has children, constantly provokes Hannah. Hannah's husband tries to console her by giving her a "double portion" of food, which only makes matters worse with the other wife.

▶ Hannah's supplication—1 Samuel 1:9-18

Though Hannah is childless, she is not prayerless. On one occasion while worshiping in the house of the Lord at Shiloh, her sorrow becomes especially intense, and Hannah weeps as she prays. She vows that if God gives her a son, she will give him back to the Lord. As she prays with her lips but not her voice, Eli, the priest, comes to think she is drunk and rebukes her. Hannah protests her innocence and proceeds to pour out her soul to Eli. Realizing her desire for a child is intense and her spirit is sacrificial in that she wants nothing for herself, Eli assures Hannah that her heartfelt prayer has been heard. Hannah then rises from prayer with renewed trust in God and a changed attitude, her sadness having departed.

▸ Hannah's son—*1 Samuel 1:19-28*

Hannah returns home, believing God is going to answer her prayer. Sure enough, before the next year's trip to the house of the Lord, Hannah gives birth to a son. When the time comes for her to do so, Hannah brings little Samuel, her only child and son, to Eli at Shiloh and leaves him there.

▸ Hannah's song—*1 Samuel 2:1-10*

Standing with her son before Eli, Hannah utters a song of thanksgiving that rivals all others in Scripture. While her earlier prayer came from bitterness (1:10), this prayer of praise comes from joy. She bursts forth into a song and pours out her gratitude to God for His goodness. The contents of her prayer later form the basis of the "Magnificat" offered up by Mary, the mother of Jesus, to the same covenant-keeping God (Luke 1:46-55).

▸ Hannah's sacrifice—*1 Samuel 2:11*

More that anything, Hannah wants a son, and when God gives her one, she fulfills her vow to give him back to the Lord. Her sacrifice is rewarded by God with the births of five more children. As for Samuel, he grows up to reflect his mother's godliness and her praying spirit. He becomes a man of prayer and intercession for God's people all his days.

The Portrait

Hannah is one of the most noble Hebrew women mentioned in the Bible. She was a woman of exceptional faith and deep commitment. Her prayer of thanksgiving recognized the power of God and the certainty of ultimate justice. It expressed faith in God's power to keep His own and joy at answered prayers. It also exuded thankfulness. Hannah's song of thanksgiving contains the first mention of the prophesied future "king" as "His anointed" (2:10). Her prayer revealed an uncommon understanding of divine things in an age when many other people seemed to have little understanding of God and even less desire to serve Him.

Life Lessons from Hannah

Hannah teaches you to pray about life's sorrows. Hannah suffered unbearably, which pressed her to God in prayer. She began her prayer with a heavy heart, but finished with a hopeful heart. Prayer will do that for you, too. Praying passes your burdens from your shoulders onto the strong shoulders of the Lord. Cast your cares on the Lord, for He cares for you.

Hannah teaches you to take time to shape the lives of your children. Hannah had only a few short years with Samuel. Yet during that brief time, she instilled in him much wisdom and knowledge about God—enough to carry him through a lifetime of devotion to God. It is never too early to start training your children in the ways of God.

Hannah teaches you to follow through on your promises. Hannah could have made many excuses for not wanting to give up her baby, her only son. But Hannah does not appear to hesitate in following through on her promise to dedicate Samuel to God's service. Make good on your promises, whether they are to God or anyone else.

Understanding the Person of God
from Hannah's Prayer (1 Samuel 2:1-10)

God is Savior—"I rejoice in Your salvation" (verse 1)

God is holy—"No one is holy like the Lord" (verse 2)

God is mighty—"Nor is there any rock like our God" (verse 2)

God is all knowing—"The Lord is the God of knowledge" (verse 3)

God is powerful—"The pillars of the earth are the Lord's and He has set the world upon them" (verse 8)

God is caring—"He will guard the feet of His saints" (verse 9)

God is Judge—"The adversaries of the Lord shall be broken in pieces" (verse 10)

Samuel

The Last Judge

*So the children of Israel said to Samuel, "Do not
cease to cry out to the LORD our God for us, that
He may save us from the hand of the Philistines."*
1 SAMUEL 7:8

☙

Most notable quality: Man of faith and prayer
Most notable accomplishment: Oversaw transition from
judges to monarchy
Date lived: 1105–1030 B.C.
Name: *Samuel*, meaning "name of God"
Major text: 1 Samuel 1–8

Bare Bones Background

As Samuel arrives on the scene, Israel is at a low point spiritually.
The priesthood is lead by Eli, a well-meaning man who, as a parent, can't
control his two corrupt sons. Politically, Israel's different tribes have their
own leadership. Occasionally, during desperate times, judges are raised
up by God to give leadership, but basically there is no working together
as a nation. The people are therefore easily controlled by other nations,
such as the Philistines, who had mastered the use of iron and controlled
its supply, which gives them a decided military advantage. In addition,
the ark of the covenant, built by Moses, had been irreverently taken
from the tabernacle and allowed to fall into the hands of the Philistines,
and idolatry was widespread.

Quick Sketch

During his lifetime, Samuel will become Israel's greatest judge, and will also function as a priest and a prophet. During his years as a judge, the loosely connected tribes are able to gain and maintain a degree of independence from their greatest enemy, the Philistines. Samuel is given the responsibility by God of overseeing the transition from a loose association of tribes into a unified kingdom with a single king. Samuel anoints Saul as Israel's first king and serves as his adviser during the early years of his reign. When Saul fails to obey God, Samuel will be sent by God to anoint David as Saul's successor.

The Big Picture

▶ **Samuel's heritage**—*1 Samuel 1:1–2:11*

Hannah, the mother of Samuel, is one of the two wives of Elkanah, a member of the tribe of Levi. Being of a priestly heritage, Samuel will later legally qualify to perform sacrifices as a priest.

▶ **Samuel's early life at the tabernacle**—*1 Samuel 2:12–3:18*

After Hannah brings Samuel to the tabernacle, he comes under the care of Eli the priest. Even as a child, Samuel "ministered before the LORD" (2:18). He is daily exposed to the sacrifices and praise offerings. But he is also exposed to the corrupt practices of Eli's two sons. One of Samuel's first assignments, even as a young boy, is to inform his mentor, Eli, that God has judged Eli's family because Eli has failed to restrain his wicked sons.

▶ **Samuel's challenge to all Israel**—*1 Samuel 7:1-9*

After Eli and his sons die as a result of judgment from God, Samuel becomes the recognized spiritual leader of Israel. The people know Samuel has a close relationship with God and are motivated to return to the Lord because they know Samuel would pray for them if they returned. They have confidence in the power of his prayers for them.

▶ **Samuel leads Israel to victory**—*1 Samuel 7:10-14*

One of the roles of the judges of ancient Israel was to free God's people from foreign oppressors. Samuel proves to be such a leader as he prays for the people and they become courageous. They fight the invading Philistines, and God provides the victory. The Philistines do not threaten Israel again until the end of Samuel's life.

▶ Samuel's jealousy for God's honor—*1 Samuel 8:1-22*

During the era of the judges, God was viewed as Israel's King. Israel was a theocracy, a nation ruled by God. When Samuel is old, he tries to make his sons judges. Tragically, Samuel's sons had not followed their father and proved to be corrupt and ungodly. Israel rejects Samuel's sons, and instead asks for a human king like those of the nations around them. Samuel tries to discourage their request as a bad idea, but finally the Lord tells Samuel to do as the people ask. They had not rejected Samuel, but God.

▶ Samuel anoints Israel's first kings—*1 Samuel 9–16*

God clearly identifies Saul to Samuel as the man to be anointed king. Saul was impressive—literally, he stood head and shoulders above all the other men. Even though Saul is to be Samuel's successor, Samuel has a deep affection for him. But Saul quickly proves to be a great disappointment, disobeying God's commands on different occasions. Finally, God sends Samuel to Saul with the message that the Lord had rejected him. God next sends Samuel to Bethlehem and the house of Jesse, where he anoints young David to succeed Saul.

▶ Samuel's Death—*1 Samuel 25:1*

Samuel mourns the rebellious self-interests of Saul. Samuel had always had the people's interest at heart, and he is heartbroken to see the flaws in his successor. It isn't too long after Saul is rejected by God that Samuel dies. The death of Samuel, the last of the judges, was the end of an era that spanned about 350 years from the conquest under Joshua until the establishment of the monarchy. So widespread was Samuel's influence that all Israel gathers to mourn his death.

The Portrait

Samuel's godliness and commitment are nurtured even before his birth, as his godly mother, Hannah, dedicates her yet-to-be-born son to the Lord. Hannah's passion for God and her vow undoubtedly was passed on to

Samuel during his first two to three years of childhood before being left to serve God at the tabernacle. From his early youth, Samuel's prophetic words came true and he became established as an authentic spokesman for God. He was a man who did not cease to pray for the people (1 Samuel 7:5,8). His burning desire was that the people would return to the Lord. His close relationship with God gave the people great confidence as they returned to serving God. As Samuel prayed, Israel became confident, and God provided a great victory over their enemy, the Philistines. Throughout his life, Samuel remained fully committed to God. In all he did, Samuel showed himself to be a man of faith and prayer. He had a marked influence on his people as they made the transition into a new form of government.

Life Lessons from Samuel

Parents have a powerful influence. Hannah dedicated her unborn son to God and she spent her child's first three years preparing him to serve God. Your love, prayers, and example will have a powerful influence on the spiritual direction of your children. View the spiritual training of your children as your highest calling. Like Hannah, start the training of your children early.

Spiritual development is nurtured by exposure to worship. Samuel spent much of his early life ministering and observing the many acts of worship conducted at the tabernacle. The earlier you teach your children about God and expose them to God's people at your local church, the more willing they will be to respond when God speaks to them through the preaching and teaching that takes place at that church.

Spiritual growth involves personal choices. Samuel was exposed to the godly ways of Eli, and the ungodly ways of Eli's two sons. Samuel chose to take his stand with God. You too have choices to make as to your level of commitment to God. Choose to follow God, and you will grow spiritually.

More Facts About Samuel

- Samuel's sons were Joel and Abijah
- High point—the return of the people to the Lord
- Low point—the people's rejection of God as King

Saul

Israel's First King

*For rebellion is as the sin of divination, and
insubordination is as iniquity and idolatry.
Because you [Saul] have rejected the word of the
LORD, He has also rejected you from being king.*

1 SAMUEL 15:23 (NASB)

Most notable quality: Strong outward appearance
Most notable accomplishment: Keeps the kingdom unified
Date lived: 70 years (reigned 40 years, from 1051 B.C. to 1011 B.C.)
Name: *Saul*, meaning "asked"
Major text: 1 Samuel 9–31

Bare Bones Background

The tiny nation of Israel is on the upswing. The prophet Samuel has
led the country into spiritual renewal. His prayers and commitment to
God have inspired the people to defeat an invading force of Philistines.
Now the people are feeling a sense of national pride and want a change.
They believe that a king would give them an advantage in battle. They
reject Samuel's corrupt sons as their leaders and ask for a human
king, like those of the nations around them. Samuel is annoyed, not for
himself, but for the honor of God. Up until now, Israel had been led by
God through judges. But God tells Samuel to give the people their king.
Samuel is charged with anointing the nation's first king, a 30-year-old
man by the name of Saul, from the tribe of Benjamin.

Quick Sketch

Saul is just what the people want—a physically imposing man who stands head and shoulders above all others. After his coronation, he achieves early military victories that solidify his support among the people. But all too soon, Saul begins to collapse under the pressure of leadership. This breakdown comes because of Saul's inability to trust God and an unwillingness to obey God. Samuel tries to work with Saul. It wasn't that Saul couldn't get things right, it was that he wouldn't do things right. God rejects Saul as ruler, but Saul continues to rule, going on to reign for a total of 40 years. A bright spot in Saul's life is his oldest son, Jonathan, who became a close friend and defender of David. Jonathan is a stabilizing force both in the palace and on the battlefield. In the end, Saul and three of his sons, including Jonathan, die in a battle against the Philistines. With their king dead, the army flees from the battlefield in defeat.

The Big Picture

▶ **Saul's beginnings as king**—*1 Samuel 9–12*

The smallest tribe of Israel, the tribe of Benjamin, provides the first king for Israel. Saul is around 30 years old and in charge of caring for his father's land and herds. While out searching for lost livestock, Saul is met and anointed as king by Samuel, who had been told the day before, by God, that Saul was the man God had appointed as king. Saul passes his first military test by defeating an invading army of Ammonites. Taking advantage of Saul's popularity, Samuel calls the people together and challenges them to renew their covenant with God.

▶ **Saul's acts of disobedience**—*1 Samuel 13; 15*

In Saul's second year as king, Israel is again threatened, this time by the Philistines, who have a much larger military force made up of chariots, horsemen, and soldiers. Saul endeavors to rally the men to battle, and a meager 3000 men respond to his call. Earlier, Samuel had directed Saul to meet him in seven days so that Samuel could offer sacrifices to the Lord. On the seventh day, Samuel had not arrived. Fearing potential defeat as more and more men are lost to desertion, Saul determines to offer the sacrifice himself, even though he is not a priest. Soon Samuel arrives and condemns Saul for acting "foolishly" (verse 13) and announces that Saul's family would not be allowed to continue his kingdom dynasty.

Samuel next sends Saul to wipe out a group called the Amalekites, along with all their herds. Against God's command, Saul allows their king to live and keeps some of their cattle and other valuables as spoil. When confronted by Samuel, Saul first lies and says he had planned to offer the cattle up for sacrifices. Then he excuses himself by pleading that his fear of the people of Israel caused him to act this way. Finally, Saul admits that he has sinned against the Lord, and asks that his sin be kept secret. Instead of giving a humble confession before the nation, Saul asks Samuel to "honor me" before the people (1 Samuel 15:30). He is again rebuked by Samuel.

▶ Saul's instability—*1 Samuel 16:14-31*

With the rejection of Saul and the anointing of David, the Spirit of God departs from Saul and a dark spirit comes upon him. He becomes jealous of David, who is now one of his officers, and tries to kill him. David flees for his life. In his paranoia, Saul fears David and makes numerous attempts to kill him. Near the end of his life, with Samuel now dead and silence from God, Saul goes to a spirit medium for answers. To the surprise of the medium, Samuel's spirit miraculously appears and informs Saul that his disobedience will lead to his and his sons' deaths the next day in battle. Just as predicted by the spirit of Samuel, Saul and his three oldest sons die the next day.

The Portrait

The life of Saul is a sad illustration of the consequences of unrepentant sin. When we first meet Saul, he is a physically impressive man. After his anointing, the Spirit of God came upon him and he initially enjoyed success. But then he began to make bad decisions, blaming others for his actions and acting out of fear and self-interest. Then when he was confronted, he refused to repent. As a result, God withdrew His blessing and Spirit from Saul. Now spiritually adrift, Saul plunged further into jealousy, fear, paranoia, disobedience, and ultimately, suicide—Saul's final expression of his faithless condition.

Life Lessons from Saul

Saul's life shows the importance of inner character. From all outward appearances, Saul looked the part of a king, but inwardly, Saul had numerous character flaws. Saul's life reminds you not to be obsessed with your outward appearance. Instead, be obsessed with developing your inner person, your character. Spend time reading God's Word and asking God to eliminate any bad habits in your life and, in their place, instill good ones.

Saul's life shows the importance of obedience. Saul was unwilling to do things God's way. He always had a better idea and, when confronted, he always had excuses or justifications for his wrong actions. God doesn't want your excuses or your rationalizations. Are there any areas of your life in which you are failing to submit to God's rule? God wants complete obedience—give it to Him now!

Saul's life shows the importance of confession. Saul's downfall began with unconfessed sin. Confession is agreeing with God that you have fallen short of His perfect standard in some way. Don't let sin get a foothold in your life. Your continued usefulness to a holy God requires that you are continually confessing your sins.

More Facts About Saul

First king of Israel, from the tribe of Benjamin

Lived 70 years

Father: Kish

Wife: Ahinoam

Sons: Jonathan, Abinadab (Ishva), Malkishua, Ish-Bosheth

Daughters: Merab, Michal (David's first wife)

David

Sweet Psalmist of Israel

*When He [God] had removed him [Saul], He
raised up for them David as king, to whom
also He gave testimony and said, "I have
found David the son of Jesse, a man after
My own heart, who will do all My will."*
ACTS 13:22

☘

Most notable quality: Heart for God
Most notable accomplishment: Unified Israel
Date lived: 1040–970 B.C. (lived 70 years)
Name: *David*, meaning "beloved"
Major text: 1 Samuel 16–1 Kings 2

Bare Bones Background

After the death of Saul, David is crowned king by the tribe of Judah, which was in the southern part of Israel. After seven years of civil war, David is anointed king over all Israel. During the reign of David, the great empires of Egypt to the south and Babylon and Assyria to the north are in varying states of weakness. They will present no threat to Israel during the years of David's 40-year reign. The only real threats will be the Philistines to the west and the Ammonites to the east.

Quick Sketch

David, like his predecessor, Saul, is of humble background. Yet he will rise to become the greatest king in the history of Israel. He is a born leader and forges an army that makes the tiny nation of Israel the most powerful Middle Eastern kingdom of his era. He establishes Jerusalem both as the political capital and the religious center of the nation, and brings the ark of God to Jerusalem. He is a gifted poet, with 73 of his poems included in the book of Psalms.

In spite of his excellent gifts and abilities, David still falls prey to temptation and sin. God forgives him, but his family and kingdom never recover from the consequences of his adulterous sin with Bathsheba.

The Big Picture

▶ **David as a shepherd**—*1 Samuel 16*

David is the youngest of the eight sons of Jesse and lives in Bethlehem, about six miles from Jerusalem, the future site of David's capital. As the youngest son, David is assigned to watch over the sheep. During these early days and nights while alone in the fields, David develops a reverence for God. This respect for God as Creator often found its way into his psalms, such as Psalm 19. It is during these shepherd days that Samuel anoints David, still a teenager, as God's second king. Saul continues as king, but God has rejected him and God's Spirit leaves Saul and comes mightily upon David.

▶ **David as a military hero**—*1 Samuel 17–18*

The Philistine invasion of Israel brings David to the battlefront with supplies for his older brothers, who are part of Saul's army. When David arrives, he is puzzled that no one—not even the king—is willing to fight the champion of the Philistines, a nine-foot-tall giant named Goliath. David accepts the challenge, kills the giant with a single stone from his slingshot, and from that day forward, displays continued courage and brilliance for the rest of his military career. Jonathan, Saul's eldest son, develops a close friendship with David during David's rise in popularity. David is so honored by the people that Saul begins to look upon him with suspicion and jealousy.

▸ **David as an outlaw**—*1 Samuel 19–31*

With each of David's successes, Saul becomes more jealous. Even though David is now Saul's son-in-law, having married Saul's daughter, Michal, Saul attempts to kill David. With the help of Michal and Jonathan, David flees for his life. During the remaining years until his death, Saul would often pursue David. There are many close calls and last-minute escapes. As a born leader, David assembles a band of about 600 fierce fighting men and their families. Eventually, these men will make up the core of David's army when he becomes king.

▸ **David as king over Judah**—*2 Samuel 1–4*

With the death of Saul and three of his sons, Jonathan being one of them, David is made king over Judah, his tribe of origin. He is now 30 years old. One of Saul's younger sons, Ish-bosheth, is declared king in the north, but it takes about five years for him to get all the people of the northern tribes to declare him their king. He reigns two years, then is murdered by his own men.

▸ **David as a kingdom builder**—*2 Samuel 5–10*

All of Israel now comes together and anoints David as king. David had reigned for seven years over Judah, and he will reign for 33 years over all of Israel. His first act as king is to establish a new capital by capturing Jerusalem. During the process of defeating all of Israel's foes, David will expand the borders of Israel tenfold. He also organizes the nation's government and brings the ark of the covenant, the most holy object in Israel's religion, to Jerusalem.

▸ **David's declining years**—*2 Samuel 11–24; 1 Kings 2:10*

David's faith and trust in God has brought him to the pinnacle of success. He is the most powerful man in the region. But with no more challenges, a lethargy seems to take hold of David. Rather than go out and fight one more battle, David decides to stay in Jerusalem. As he walks on his roof, he sees a beautiful woman bathing below. He sends for her, commits adultery with her, then tries to hide his sin by murdering the woman's husband.

One year later, David finally repents after being confronted by the prophet Nathan. God forgives David, but his moral failure will have a devastating effect on his family. One son rapes his half-sister, who is then killed by her brother, who later leads a rebellion that forces David to flee from Jerusalem before the son is killed in battle.

In his last years, David uses his energies and wealth preparing for the construction of a permanent temple that would replace the tabernacle, which had been a mobile place of worship to God during the exodus and the years following.

David's final act as king is to have his son, Solomon, anointed king. David then dies in bed at age 70.

The Portrait

David's life was full of contradictions:

- On the one hand, David was a deeply spiritual man with a tender heart for God, who spent much time praying, praising God, and writing psalms of worship for the Lord. On the other hand, he was a military genius who spent much of his life fighting and killing his enemies.

- One the one hand, David was intensely committed in his loyalty to Saul, even to his own peril. On the other hand, he was unconcerned about his exploitation of the women in his life.

- One the one hand, David had a great passion for honoring God and leading God's people in worship. On the other hand, he was an uninvolved father who failed to control, guide, or discipline his children.

How are we to understand David's life of contradiction?

First, we need to understand that the great David was just a man like us, with the same sin nature every person has. As you read his psalms, you see his struggles between the desire to do what was right and his inability at times to accomplish that desire. We will experience those kinds of struggles as well.

Second, God understood the imperfect nature of David's love for Him. God obviously wasn't looking for perfection. Rather, He was looking for progression. God looked into David's heart and saw a man who often failed, but still truly desired to obey Him.

Life Lessons from David

A deep relationship with God takes time to build. David spent many hours watching over his father's sheep, which allowed him much time to meditate upon and worship God. Later he would write poems (psalms) about this growing relationship. If you want to know God better, you too must spend time in personal and corporate worship.

Good friends will be there during the rough times. David and Jonathan developed a deep friendship that was mutually edifying. Their friendship was characterized by loyalty, love, and trust. This close relationship helped each of them to survive the hard times. Develop and protect those friendships that will build you up, encourage you, and challenge you in your walk with God. Seek true friends who are loyal, loving, and trustworthy.

No one is immune to temptation. David's fall came after he had experienced years of immense success, and this most likely weakened his dependence upon God. Temptation will always lurk behind the next bend in the road, looking for an opportunity to make us fail. Never allow yourself to think you no longer need God for help with everyday living. It's in the everyday living that you will need God the most.

Confession of sin is the first step to restoration. After his sin with Bathsheba, David's unrepentant heart was destroying him physically. His deep sense of guilt is described in Psalm 32. After his repentance, as expressed in Psalm 51, David's heart, health, and joy were restored. When you repent of sin and ask God's forgiveness, you will experience spiritual and physical restoration. Don't harbor sin in your life. Confess quickly, and be quickly restored.

Parenting requires involvement. David was an important, busy, and successful man. He was tops in his profession. But he failed as a father partly because of his lack of attention to the needs of his children. Parenting is a responsibility that requires much time and effort. But the rewards are great when you see your children grow up able to make right choices. Hopefully they will make the best choice of all, which is to choose Jesus as their Lord and Savior.

David's Life	Saul's Life
He was God's king (2 Samuel 7:8-16)	He was the people's king (1 Samuel 10:23)
He was a man after God's own heart (Acts 13:22)	He was a man seeking the people's praise (1 Samuel 15:30)
His reign is eternal (2 Samuel 7:12-13)	His reign was brief (1 Samuel 15:28)
He was kind and giving (2 Samuel 9)	He was harsh (1 Samuel 22:16-19)
He was forgiving (1 Samuel 26)	He was unforgiving (1 Samuel 14:24-44)
He was repentant (2 Samuel 12:13)	He was unrepentant (1 Samuel 15:10-31)
He was brave (1 Samuel 17)	He was fearful (1 Samuel 17:11)
He possessed God's Spirit (1 Samuel 16:13)	He was separated from God (1 Samuel 16:14)

Solomon

The Wisest Man on Earth

I have given you a wise and understanding heart,
so that there has not been anyone like you before
you, nor shall any like you arise after you.
1 KINGS 3:12

Most notable quality: Wisest man on earth
Most notable accomplishment: Built the first permanent temple
Date lived: Reigned 40 years, from 971 B.C. to 931 B.C.
Name: *Solomon*, meaning "peaceful"—also called Jedidiah, "beloved of the Lord," by Nathan the prophet (2 Samuel 12:25)
Major texts: 1 Kings 1–11; 2 Chronicles 1–9

Bare Bones Background

After the death of King David, the mantle of leadership passed on to Solomon. Solomon is the second king of the Davidic dynasty in Israel. God promises that this dynasty will have no end (2 Samuel 7:13). Solomon inherits a kingdom that is stable and well managed. None of the surrounding nations are strong enough to break away or cause problems. Solomon extends his control from Egypt to the Euphrates River. During his reign of 40 years, the region is at peace, with only a few minor uprisings.

Quick Sketch

Solomon is the third king of Israel and the son of David and Bathsheba. His reign of 40 years sustains the nation as a major influence in the region. His wisdom is known far and wide. He is the wisest man of his day, and a writer of thousands of proverbs. He is an aggressive builder not only of the temple, but of palaces for himself and his many wives. He maintains a large standing army of chariots, but through diplomacy, remains at peace with the surrounding nations. He is the only Hebrew king ever to maintain a fleet of trading vessels. Though wealthy beyond imagination, the kingdom is always in need of money for Solomon's lavish lifestyle and building projects. To raise money, he heavily taxes his subjects.

The Big Picture

▶ **Solomon's Rise to Power**—*1 Kings 1–2:12*

Solomon's rise to the throne is not without incident. David has failed to acknowledge Solomon as his heir, so the next son in line for the throne, Adonijah, starts making preparations for his own coronation as David lies dying.

Nathan, the prophet, and Bethsheba, Solomon's mother, remind David of his unexercised promise that Solomon would be the next king. King David gives instructions for Solomon's accession, and seals it with an oath. Still desiring the throne, Adonijah makes a proposal to Bathsheba for Abishag, David's handmaiden, that she be given to him as a wife. This act is seen as a threat to Solomon, who has Adonijah killed along with Joab, David's military general who had supported Adonijah's bid for the throne. With these apparent threats out of the way, Solomon rules without a rival.

▶ **Solomon's wisdom**—*1 Kings 3:5-28*

Realizing the enormity of his task as king, Solomon chooses an "understanding heart" (verse 9) when asked by God in a dream to choose anything he desires. The later incident with the two women claiming the same baby as their own typifies the wisdom that makes Solomon respected and feared for his justice. Solomon's verdict: Cut the baby in two pieces and give half to each woman. The woman who said no was identified as the mother and given the baby.

Solomon's wisdom inspired him to collect and compose thousands of proverbs and songs (1 Kings 4:32). Many of his wise sayings are preserved in the book of Proverbs. He also wrote the Song of Solomon, a poetic book in praise of love in marriage.

▸ Solomon's temple—*1 Kings 6*

King David had spent the latter years of his life amassing the materials for a great temple to be built for the worship of God. He charges Solomon to carry out and complete the task. The foundation is laid 480 years after the nation's exodus from Egypt, in the year 965 B.C., and the temple is completed seven years and six months later. The temple stood as a place of worship until it was destroyed by Babylonian forces under King Nebuchadnezzar in 587 B.C.

▸ Solomon's wealth—*1 Kings 10*

Trading for goods is one of King Solomon's strengths. With Israel's strategic position as a land bridge between Egypt and Asia, Solomon sets out to control the caravan routes. He also builds ships that monopolize the sea lanes. Solomon's annual income is 25 tons of gold. Because of his wealth, silver is considered as nothing during his reign (verse 21).

▸ Solomon's statesmanship—*1 Kings 3:1; 5:1*

During the temporary power vacuum between the two superpowers Egypt and Assyria, Solomon is able to maintain and even expand the large empire inherited from his father. Solomon accomplishes this by making friendly alliances with his neighbor nations, sometimes sealed by marriages and maintained by a large army that was always ready, but fought no major military campaigns.

Because of his wisdom and power, kings and queens—such as the Queen of Sheba—came to pay their respects and bring gifts (1 Kings 10:1-13).

▸ Solomon's flaw—*1 Kings 11:1-8*

Marrying foreign wives may have been right for Solomon politically, but it was spiritual suicide. These foreign marriages brought foreign religions, and in time, Solomon compromises the convictions he had expressed in his prayer at the dedication of the temple (8:23). To appease his wives, Solomon engages in the worship of their foreign deities. With this terrible breach in Solomon's covenant with the Lord, judgment will come after Solomon's death. The seeds of destruction have been planted, and the fruit of Solomon's disobedience will bear fruit in the division of the kingdom during the reign of his son and successor, Rehoboam (11:43–12:17).

The Portrait

Solomon was born with privilege: His father was the king, and he was the heir to the throne. He was granted several encounters with God through dreams. He made a good start to his reign by asking God for wisdom to rule rather than wealth and long life. God was pleased with his request and gave him wisdom, and also gave Solomon the wealth. Solomon followed through on his father's request and built the temple. His prayer at the dedication of the temple revealed a heart for God. In that dedication, he also challenged the people of Israel to walk in God's laws (1 Kings 8:61). But unlike his father David, Solomon did not remain committed to the Lord throughout his life. In his later years, Solomon's foreign wives turned his heart toward other gods. In the book of Ecclesiastes, Solomon reveals the high personal price he paid for his defection from God. The book describes the misery and hopelessness that comes from a life apart from God. Solomon's life began with great promise, but had a tragic ending.

Life Lessons from Solomon

Wisdom is to be desired above knowledge. When given the opportunity by God to ask for anything he wanted, Solomon asked for wisdom—not wealth, knowledge, or a long life. Wisdom is the ability to apply the knowledge you possess and the sense to make your life count whatever its length. Ask God for His wisdom as you make your daily decisions.

Ultimate happiness is found only in knowing God. King Solomon searched for purpose and meaning in his later life. He tried it all and had it all, and finally concluded that true meaning comes only in a relationship with God. Jesus said, "I am the way, and the truth, and the life" (John 14:6). If you have not done so, invite Jesus into your life as Savior and Lord, and experience the true meaning and purpose of your existence. Your true happiness comes from only one source—the Lord Jesus Christ.

Bad company corrupts good morals. Solomon married foreign wives for his own gratification and to forge alliances with surrounding countries. Before long, Solomon was making concessions and compromising his own faith. Ask God to give you wisdom to seek only those relationships that will keep you close to your Lord.

Solomon's wealth

Annual income: 660 talents of gold (25 tons)

Gold reserves: 200 gold shields weighing 7.5 pounds each

300 gold shields weighing 3.75 pounds each

A throne of ivory overlaid with gold

All drinking glasses in all his palaces were pure gold

Silver was considered of little value in Solomon's day

Elijah

A Fiery Prophet

O LORD, the God of Abraham, Isaac and Israel,
today let it be known that You are God in Israel
and that I am your servant and I [Elijah]
have done all these things at Your word.
1 KINGS 18:36

☘

Most notable quality: Relationship with God
Most notable accomplishment: Confronted the priests of Baal
Date lived: c. 875 B.C.
Name: *Elijah*, meaning "Yahweh is my God"
Major texts: 1 Kings 17–19; 2 Kings 1–2

Bare Bones Background

Elijah lives during a strategic time in the life of the northern kingdom of Israel. Omri has become king and built his capital on the hill of Samaria. He introduces Baal worship. After his death his son, Ahab, gives the worship of Baal official recognition by building a temple for Baal in Samaria. Encouraged by his wife, Jezebel, King Ahab then initiates an aggressive campaign to destroy all worship of God and replace it with Baal worship. Elijah is sent by God to confront Ahab and to declare to the nation that the Lord is God and there are no other gods, including Baal.

Quick Sketch

Elijah the Tishbite comes from a town called Tishbe, located east of the Jordan River. He is a fiery spokesman sent by God to confront the hostile rulers of the northern kingdom for their worship of Baal, a false Canaanite god. Elijah appears and demonstrates the power of God first by bringing a three-and-one-half-year drought, then by defeating 450 prophets of Baal in a power encounter on Mount Carmel. The people respond to the display of God's power by affirming that "the LORD, He is God!" (1 Kings 18:39). The evil attempts on the part of Ahab and Jezebel to destroy the worship of the Lord are thwarted, and while the false religious system continues to exist in Israel, the hearts of the people are turned back to God, at least for a while.

The Big Picture

▶ Elijah predicts a drought—*1 Kings 17*

The first recorded words uttered by Elizah are the declaration of a devastating drought that will come upon the people of Israel because of their defection into idolatry. The drought will last three years and six months (James 5:17), and prove that Baal, the god of rain and fertility, is powerless before the one true God. During the drought, God provides for Elijah's needs with food from ravens and the sacrificial giving of a widow, whose last bit of flour and oil are miraculously multiplied for as long as Elijah stays in her home.

▶ Elijah proposes a test—*1 Kings 18*

Near the end of the drought, God sends Elijah to Ahab to propose a power challenge between Himself and 450 of the 850 priests of Baal on Mount Carmel. Elijah summons all the people of Israel to witness this confrontation between Baal and God. After the prophets of Baal are unsuccessful in their attempts to call down fire from heaven to consume an animal sacrifice, Elijah prays, and fire descends from heaven and consumes not only the sacrifice but also the stones of the altar and the water surrounding the altar. The people respond to God's demonstration of power by seizing and killing all 450 false prophets. Elijah again prays, and the drought is lifted and rain comes (James 5:17-18).

▶ **Elijah prospers from God's intervention**—*1 Kings 19*

When Queen Jezebel hears that 450 of her priests have been killed, she sends a death threat to the prophet. Even though Elijah has just prevailed over 450 priests with God's help, he is now terrified and flees for his life, traveling 100 miles. Viewing his situation as hopeless, Elijah asks God to take his life. But God provides bread and water and a touch from the Angel of the Lord. These help sustain Elijah for a 40-day journey to Mount Sinai where God...

- communicates His care—God speaks to Elijah in a "still small voice" (verse 12)

- provides a new companion—Elisha, who will be Elijah's friend, companion, and successor (verse 16)

- supplies a new task—Elijah is to anoint two kings who will bring an end to Ahab's evil family (verses 15-17)

- delivers a new perspective—Elijah is not alone, for 7000 people have not bowed their knees to Baal (verse 18)

The Portrait

Elijah was a man dedicated to God in a hostile society. He was bold and brave, but he was also human and susceptible to fear and depression. At the moment of his greatest victory, the confrontation with the 450 priests of Baal, Elijah was frightened by the threats of Queen Jezebel. God dealt with his prophet's depression in a gracious way, never rebuking him, only ministering to and nurturing him back to usefulness.

Elijah had his faltering moments, but he was always devoted to God. God acknowledged Elijah's dedication by taking him to heaven alive in a chariot of fire with horses of fire (2 Kings 2:11). Elijah was the second person mentioned in Scripture who was taken to heaven without dying (Enoch was the first—Genesis 5:21-24).

Life Lessons from Elijah

You are never alone in the battle. However alone you may feel today, be reminded that many others love God as much as you do. Elijah thought he alone was the defender of God's cause, and God assured him that 7000 others in the nation had not bowed their knees to false gods. You are not alone. Seek fellowship in your local church with other likeminded believers.

Be bold even in the midst of a faithless society. Armed only with the boldness of God, Elijah singlehandedly challenged 450 prophets of Baal. On occasions when you too are surrounded by unbelief, be courageous and speak up for God. As was the case with Elijah, God will be honored by your boldness.

Everyone is susceptible to bouts of fear and depression. Even though Elijah was wholeheartedly committed to the Lord, he still experienced a time of discouragement. God then sustained and encouraged Elijah and sent him back into the battle. God is likewise committed to you today, and even in your hour of discouragement, He knows your pain and will meet your needs.

Elijah's Life of Miracles

He prays, and a drought comes (1 Kings 17:1).

He is fed by ravens (1 Kings 17:1-7).

He and a widow are sustained for months on a little flour and oil (1 Kings 17:8-16).

He raises the widow's son from the dead (1 Kings 17:17-24).

He prays, and fire consumes an altar and the sacrifice upon it (1 Kings 18:20-40).

He prays, and rain comes (1 Kings 18:41-45).

He prays, and fire consumes the king's men (2 Kings 1:1-17).

He divides and walks through the Jordan River (2 Kings 2:6-8).

He is taken to heaven in a chariot of fire (2 Kings 2:9-12).

Elisha
The People's Prophet

*Elijah said to Elisha, "Ask what I shall
do for you before I am taken from you."
And Elisha said,"Please, let a double
portion of your spirit be upon me."*
2 KINGS 2:9 (NASB)

☙

Most notable quality: Compassion for the people
Most notable accomplishment: Successor to Elijah
Date lived: 867–797 B.C. (lived 70 years)
Name: *Elisha*, meaning "God is salvation"
Major text: 1 Kings 19:16–2 Kings 13:20

Bare Bones Background

From the time of the division of Israel into two kingdoms, the
northern kingdom has had a succession of evil kings, each being more
wicked than the last. God will judge the northern kingdom for its sin of
idolatry. Elisha is called into prophetic ministry about 120 years before
God destroys the kingdom. His purpose is to restore respect for God
and His message. This will be done by a succession of miracles that
show that God controls not only great armies, but also the events of
everyday life.

Quick Sketch

Elisha has a very different ministry than that of Elijah. Elijah's role was confrontational during a time of great apostasy. Elisha, his successor, focuses his ministry and miracles on the needs of the people of the northern kingdom, Israel. Elisha's miracles reveal God's gracious nature to nations, individuals, and even to a foreign general.

The Big Picture

Elisha, Elijah's understudy, asks his mentor, Elijah, for a "double portion" of his spirit (2 Kings 2:9). Elisha's purpose in asking for this is so that he could continue the work of his teacher. God seems to have honored Elisha's request because Scripture records seven miracles performed by Elijah and 14 performed by Elisha. The miracles done by Elisha demonstrate God's desire to bless the entire nation if they would simply turn back to Him:

1. Elisha divides the Jordan River (2 Kings 2:14)

2. Elisha purifies bitter springs of water (2:21)

3. Elisha brings a curse on men who ridiculed God (2:24)

4. Elisha predicts a miraculous victory for Israel (3:15-26)

5. Elisha multiplies a poor widow's oil (4:1-7)

6. Elisha promises a son to a kind woman (4:14-17)

7. Elisha raises the kind woman's dead son (4:32-37)

8. Elisha makes poisonous stew edible (4:38-41)

9. Elisha multiplies loaves of bread to feed many (4:42-44)

10. Elisha heals a proud general of leprosy (5:1-19)

11. Elisha floats a borrowed ax head (6:1-6)

12. Elisha shows his servant an army of angels (6:15-17)

13. Elisha blinds an army sent to capture him (6:8-23)

14. Elisha predicts the lifting of the siege of Samaria and an excess of food for the starving people (6:24–7:20)

The Portrait

Elisha had a less spectacular ministry than that of Elijah, but it wasn't any less important. Elisha's ministry was to the people, not their rulers. His actions are a reflection of his gentle, loving nature, and his miracles reveal God's love, care, and concern for the needs of the less fortunate. Elisha began his ministry as Elijah's understudy and servant. As the time approached for Elijah's departure, Elisha asked for a "double portion" of Elijah's power, not from a desire for power or fame. Elisha was asking to succeed his mentor in the prophetic office with spiritual powers beyond his own ability. He realized the enormous responsibilities that lay ahead of him, and desired that Elijah's mighty power might continue to live through him. His request was a noble one and God granted him 50-plus years of dynamic ministry, with a life that spanned the reigns of kings from Ahab to Joash.

Life Lessons from Elisha

Elisha's life teaches the importance of commitment. From the hour that Elijah threw his mantle over Elisha while plowing in a field, Elisha focuses his life on serving Elijah and God. To show his break from family, he slaughters the oxen he has been plowing with and gives a farewell feast for his family. God may not be calling you to a high-profile public ministry, but He is asking you to be fully devoted to Him wherever life finds you. A commitment to God also means a commitment to the people of God.

Elisha's life teaches that a disciple not only learns from his teacher, but also builds upon what he has learned. Elisha became Elijah's constant companion and understudy. He followed and served Elijah completely. He was a good student and follower, and when it was his turn to lead, Elisha became an effective replacement for Elijah. Today, discipleship is God's way of training you for effective service. Find someone who is serving effectively and ask to learn from him. When you have learned what you need to know and do, build upon that learning and pass it on to others.

Elisha's life teaches that all ministry is significant. Elisha had a less spectacular ministry than that of Elijah. But in the economy of God, it was significant in its revelation of God's love for His people. You have been called and gifted by God, and are not to measure yourself against other people or the scope of their ministries. The role you play in God's plan is the role He has designed for you, and that makes you significant. Be faithful to fulfill your role as Elisha did his. Your life is significant. Live it wisely!

More Facts About Elisha

- He was from the area of Gilead, east of the Jordan River
- He prophesied to the northern kingdom
- His life and ministry to the northern kingdom spanned the reigns of six kings (Ahab, Ahaziah, Jehoram, Jehu, Jehoahaz, Jehoash)

Hezekiah
Faithful to the Lord in Everything

Thus Hezekiah did...what was good and right and true before the LORD his God. And in every work that he began in the service of the house of God, in the law and in the commandment, to seek his God, he did it with all his heart. So he prospered.
2 CHRONICLES 31:20-21

☩

Most notable quality: Trust in God
Most notable accomplishment: His prayers preserved Judah from an invasion
Date lived: 740 B.C.–686 B.C. (lived 54 years)
Name: *Hezekiah*, meaning "Yahweh is my strength"
Major texts: 2 Kings 18–20; 2 Chronicles 29–32; Isaiah 36–39

Bare Bones Background

When Hezekiah became king, the great Assyrian Empire was pushing its way toward the tiny nation of Judah. Israel to the north—along with its capital, Samaria—had fallen, and its inhabitants had been deported to Assyria. Hezekiah inherits a nation rampant in gross idolatry and poverty. His father, Ahaz, was the first king in the line of David to institute pagan worship on the "high places." Ahaz also places his allegiance in foreign kings and drains the nation dry paying tribute to these powers for protection—all the while turning his back on God.

Quick Sketch

Within one year of assuming the throne, Hezekiah begins an aggressive campaign to undo all the spiritual damage done by his father. He reopens the temple, removes the high places of pagan worship, destroys all sacred pillars and idolatrous images, and reinstitutes the religious festivals. He refuses to submit to Assyria, and when Assyria invades Judah, Hezekiah prays and God miraculously intervenes. Hezekiah then becomes ill and God answers his prayer of devotion and grants him an additional 15 years of life. God continues to bless Hezekiah's devotion, and Judah becomes a prosperous nation. Hezekiah's fame causes him to become proud, and he foolishly displays the nation's wealth to the son of the king of Babylon. He is rebuked by the prophet Isaiah for exercising such poor judgment. Upon Hezekiah's death, his son, Manasseh, reigns in his place.

The Big Picture

▶ **Hezekiah's focus is on worship**—*2 Chronicles 29–31*

In the first year of his reign, Hezekiah reopens the temple for worship, which had been closed during the reign of his evil father. He immediately calls all the people to come to Jerusalem to celebrate the seven-day celebration of the Passover. This important religious festival had not been observed for many years. The joy is so great that the celebration is extended an additional seven days. The people respond by returning to their homes and destroying the idols and shrines that have polluted the land.

▶ **Hezekiah's prayers are for the honor of God**—*2 Kings 18:9–19:37; 2 Chronicles 32:1-23; Isaiah 36–37*

In Hezekiah's fourteenth year of rule, a massive Assyrian army invades Judah and surrounds Jerusalem. A message from Sennacherib, the Assyrian king, scoffs at Hezekiah's trust in God and boasts that no nation and their gods have been able to stand against his mighty power. Jerusalem too will fall, and her God will be powerless to save the people. Hezekiah takes the message before the Lord. He prays that God would affirm His power and not allow His name to be held in such contempt.

Hezekiah's prayer is answered and that same night, 185,000 Assyrian soldiers die in their sleep. The Assyrian king retreats in shame and defeat.

▸ **Hezekiah's dying request is answered**—*2 Kings 20:1-11; Isaiah 38*

Shortly after God's defeat of the Assyrian army, Hezekiah becomes deathly ill. The prophet Isaiah tells him to put his house in order before he dies. As Isaiah is leaving, Hezekiah begins to pray, asking God to remember his piety and devotion. Hezekiah doesn't specifically asked to be healed, but God responds by giving him an additional 15 years of life. Hezekiah asked for a sign to indicate whether he should "go up to the house of the LORD," so God turned back the shadow of the sun ten degrees as his sign (2 Kings 20:8-11).

▸ **Hezekiah's pride is rebuked**—*2 Kings 20:12-19; Isaiah 39*

Hearing the news of Hezekiah's miraculous healing, the son of the king of the emerging nation of Babylon comes to pay his respects and bring gifts and ask for Hezekiah's help against the still-powerful Assyrians. Hezekiah foolishly shows off his nation's wealth to this important emissary. Isaiah rebukes the king and predicts that in the future, Babylon will destroy Israel. The prediction was fulfilled in 586 B.C. with the destruction of Jerusalem and the deportation of its people.

The Portrait

Hezekiah's character stands in sharp contrast to that of Ahaz, his father. Ahaz believed in the gods of other nations. He trusted that they would be a source of power, strength, and protection for him and the nation. Hezekiah, on the other hand, is one of only very few kings whom God compares favorably with King David. More than any other king, Hezekiah brought about major spiritual reformation.

For all of Hezekiah's sterling qualities, he lacked an important one—a vision for the future spiritual well-being of the nation. It appears that he took few steps to preserve the effects of his sweeping reforms. And worse, he failed to pass on his passion for God to his son, Manasseh, who became one of the most wicked kings of Judah. Manasseh's sins and occult practices accelerated the ultimate destruction of Judah.

Life Lessons from Hezekiah

Make worship a priority in your life—Hezekiah's emphasis on worship restored Judah to a place were God could and did bless the land. Don't let the world crowd God out of your life. Do whatever is necessary to insure that personal and corporate worship are a nonnegotiable part of your life.

Pray expecting God to answer—Hezekiah's prayers for both the nation and his personal well-being were answered in wondrous ways. Hezekiah provides a powerful example of the efficacy of prayer offered by a man or woman in a right relationship with God. Walk by God's Spirit and pray fervently, and expect your prayers to have a great effect (James 5:16).

Be willing to respond as you read God's Word—Hezekiah was committed to following the commands of Scripture and the words of the prophet Isaiah. Today, you too have an opportunity to heed God's Word. Read the Bible with a sensitive, open heart. The Lord is speaking. Are you listening?

Remember that the future will determine how successful your efforts are today—King Hezekiah was very successful in establishing the supremacy of God in the land. But he failed to see his religious zeal in light of the future. He failed to make provisions for the continued protection of the spiritual condition of the people, which included training up his son in the ways of God. Your spiritual influence is not measured by today, but by how well your life and zeal for God last into the future, which includes the training of your children in the ways of God.

Kings Who Followed David's Example

Asa—"Asa did what was right in the eyes of the LORD" (1 Kings 15:11).

Hezekiah—"He did what was right in the sight of the LORD" (2 Kings 18:3).

Josiah—"He did what was right in the sight of the LORD" (2 Kings 22:2).

Job

A Blameless and Upright Man

The LORD said to Satan, "Have you
considered My servant Job? For there
is no one like him on the earth,
a blameless and upright man, fearing
God and turning away from evil."
JOB 1:8 (NASB)

☖

Most notable quality: Blameless and upright
Most notable accomplishment: Endured intense suffering
Date lived: Time of Abraham (approximately 2000 B.C.)
Name: *Job*, meaning "persecuted one"
Major text: Book of Job

Bare Bones Background

Job lives in Uz, an area near Midian, where Moses would later live 40 years as a shepherd. In the book that bears Job's name, there are no references to the law of Moses or any of the covenants that God makes with any of the Hebrew patriarchs. Also, Job conducts priestly functions on behalf of his family and lives to be nearly 200 years old. All these factors suggest that Job lives around the same time as Abraham, the father of the Hebrew nation.

Quick Sketch

Job is a godly man who has lived a trouble-free and prosperous life for many years. He is wealthy and influential and owns large herds of sheep, oxen, and camels. He is a loving husband and the caring father of seven sons and three daughters. One day, within the span of a few hours, his children and his wealth are taken away by traumatic disasters and marauding thieves. To make matters even worse, he is afflicted with painful boils from head to foot. Job is left with nothing but his faith in God, and questions as to why these calamities have befallen him. Friends come to grieve with him, but soon their comfort turns to accusations and debate. Finally, God intervenes with His perspective and His rebuke of Job's friends. The story ends with Job's restoration to happiness and wealth.

The Big Picture

▶ Job is tested—*Job 1–2*

Job is a wealthy man who loves God and is upright in character. In a scene from heaven, Satan accuses Job of following God only because God has blessed his life. God allows Satan to destroy all of Job's family and possessions to affirm that Job's devotion is not on account of these things. Sure enough, Job persists in his devotion to God. Satan then states that if Job's health is taken away, then Job will surely deny God. But in spite of being afflicted with boils from head to foot, Job continues to trust in God.

▶ Job is accused—*Job 3–37*

In a series of debates, Job's friends wrongfully assume that Job's suffering is a result of some sin he committed. They try to persuade Job to repent. With each round of debate, Job argues that he has not sinned enough to deserve such suffering, and with each denial, their accusations become more harsh.

▶ Job is confronted by God—*Job 38–41*

God Himself finally answers Job out of a whirlwind. Instead of answering Job's question about why he is suffering, God asks Job a series of questions that no human could possibly answer. Job then recognizes that God, who is all-powerful, acts in ways that he can't always understand, but that are always for his ultimate best.

▶ **Job is blessed**—*Job 42*

In response to God's confrontation, Job humbles himself. God then rebukes Job's friends for adding to Job's suffering by their false accusations and critical spirits. Job is then given double his former wealth and a new family of seven sons and three daughters.

The Portrait

Job never learned why God permitted him to suffer. But Job did learn to accept his situation without questioning God's wisdom and judgment. The Job who persevered through this ordeal knew God better and trusted Him more deeply than the Job who entered it. In the Bible, Job is mentioned along with Noah and Daniel as a righteous man (Ezekiel 14:14-20). He is again mentioned in the New Testament as an encouragement to those who are suffering despite living righteously (James 5:11).

Life Lessons from Job

Suffering is part of living. Job lived much of his life free of trouble. He did not anticipate or appreciate when his opportunity to suffer arrived. Suffering is something no one wants but everyone experiences. God never promises his children a carefree life. But what God does offer in the midst of your trouble is His grace to see you through your difficulty. Trust God, who is loving and has allowed your pain for your good.

Suffering helps you learn patience. Job learned patience as he endured his suffering. He trusted God and never gave up on God—even when his wife wanted him to curse God and die. Stay close to God, and He will give you the strength to endure even the greatest of difficulties. He will see you through what may seem to be your darkest hour.

Suffering must be seen from a divine perspective. God is at work in ways that you often will not understand. These perplexing times provide opportunities for you to strengthen your faith in the wisdom of God.

Who else did God speak to directly?

Besides Job, God spoke directly to these Old Testament people:

Adam and Eve	Cain
Noah	Abraham
Jacob	Moses
Miriam	Aaron
Samuel	Joshua
Jeremiah	Isaiah
Ezekiel	

Ezra
The Faithful Teacher

*Ezra had prepared his heart to seek the
Law of the LORD, and to do it, and to teach
statutes and ordinances in Israel.*
EZRA 7:10

☙

Most notable quality: Commitment to God's Word
Most notable accomplishment: Led the people of Israel
back to godly living
Date lived: c. 450 B.C.
Name: *Ezra*, meaning "Yahweh helps"
Major texts: Ezra 7–10; Nehemiah 8

Bare Bones Background

Babylon, the once-powerful nation that had destroyed Jerusalem
and carried the Jews into captivity, has itself been defeated by a new
world power, Persia. Ezra is a priest living in exile in a land now controlled by Persia. Under Persia's new foreign policy, captive peoples are
allowed to return to their homeland. It has been about 80 years since
a first group of exiles chose to return to their homeland of Israel to
rebuild the temple. A new king of Persia now authorizes Ezra to lead a
second group back to Jerusalem. The king even offers large amounts
of gold and silver to be taken back with Ezra to help beautify the newly
completed temple.

Quick Sketch

From the beginning of Ezra's commissioning to lead a second group of Jews back to Jerusalem, he leads by example. He demonstrates his trust in God both to the king of Persia and to his group of returnees by praying and fasting before beginning the perilous journey to Jerusalem. Once he arrives in his homeland, he is disheartened over the people's disobedience. They have married pagan women, and are lacking in public prayer and confession of sins. He has been given the authority to administer God's law even by force if necessary (7:25), but rather than force conformity to God's law, Ezra begins to pray for God to work in the lives of the people. They respond and admit their sins and agree to devise a plan to deal with their problems. This initial effort on Ezra's part sets the stage for what will later be accomplished when another leader, Nehemiah, joins Ezra. Together they will begin a revival that spreads to the entire nation.

The Big Picture

▶ Ezra's Focus—*Ezra 7*

The normal function of the priests is to minister the sacrifices in the temple. But since the deportation of the Jewish people under the Babylonians and the destruction of the temple some 150 years earlier, the priests, and especially Ezra, have taken on the ministry of teaching. Ezra personally has faithfully dedicated himself to "seek the law of the LORD, and to do it, and to teach" it (Ezra 7:10).

▶ Ezra's Faith—*Ezra 8*

Ezra receives permission to return to Jerusalem with about 7000 to 8000 men, women, and children. He is also commissioned by the Persian rulers to take back a large amount of gold and silver to be used to decorate the newly completed temple. The return trip will take the group through dangerous land, but Ezra chooses not to ask for a military escort. Rather, he determines to trust in God's help alone, and he and his fellow travelers "fasted and entreated our God" for His protection (8:23).

▶ Ezra's Finding—*Ezra 9*

When Ezra and the people arrive, he discovers that some of the Jews, including priests and Levites (the religious leaders) have intermarried with their pagan neighbors. Ezra is deeply saddened. These are some of the same sins that have driven the people from the land in the past. Rather than rant and rave, Ezra chooses to again pray and fast, confessing his shame and the sins of God's people.

▶ Ezra's Effect—*Ezra 10*

Ezra's obvious disappointment and his prayers move the people so much that soon they too are weeping and confessing their sins. The offenders voluntarily determine to separate from their pagan wives and to faithfully follow the Lord.

▶ Ezra's Explanation of God's Word—*Nehemiah 8*

Later, after Nehemiah arrives from Babylon and helps with rebuilding the wall around Jerusalem, Ezra is asked by the people to give a public reading and explanation of the law of God. For six hours every day for seven days, Ezra and other priests read and instruct the people in God's Word. The people react to the teaching by weeping tears of sorrow, conviction, and repentance. Ezra's life efforts of studying, practicing, and teaching are realized as the people respond to the reading of God's Word.

The Portrait

Long before the Persian king commissioned Ezra to lead a group of returnees back to Jerusalem, God had been preparing Ezra for this assignment. First, as a scribe, Ezra had devoted himself to carefully studying God's Word. Second, he determined to personally apply and obey what he was learning from God's Word. Third, Ezra desired to teach others to know and obey God's Word. With these priorities, it's no surprise that Ezra had such a great impact on the people of Jerusalem and ultimately the whole country. Ezra was a living example of what God wanted for His people. Ezra modeled godliness, and it was contagious. There was a great revival under his spiritual leadership.

Life Lessons from Ezra

Studying and obeying God's Word are essential to your spiritual growth. Ezra's achievements can be directly attributed to his commitment to live his life by the standards in God's Word. In order to do that, Ezra studied God's Word seriously and applied it faithfully. Ezra's example is still appropriate today. Your growing relationship with God through the study of His Word should be seen as a priority for your spiritual life. What place of priority does the study of God's Word, prayer, and worship hold in your life? What changes can you make today to guard your time alone with God? Spiritual growth is impossible without it.

Trust God with all aspects of your life. Ezra relied on the power of God to protect him during his dangerous journey to Jerusalem. Ezra also trusted God to work in the hearts of the disobedient people he encountered upon arriving in Jerusalem. What areas of your life are you failing to commit into the all-powerful hands of God? Ezra trusted God, and so should you. You are in good hands with God.

Hold fast to the authority of Scripture. Ezra was unwilling to compromise the truths taught in God's Word. To Ezra, the Scriptures were not open for reinterpretation. You too are to hold fast to the authority of God's Word, starting with your own life. Is there any area of your life in which you are attempting to "reinterpret" Scripture so as to excuse your actions? God's Word is perfectly clear. Accept its authority in your own life, and then model its authority to others. Your example is often more effective than your teaching. God's teachings are sometimes better caught than taught.

The Three Returns to Jerusalem

Order	Date	Reference	Leader	Persian King
First	538 B.C.	Ezra 1–6	Zerubbabel	Cyrus
Second	458 B.C.	Ezra 7–10	Ezra	Artaxerxes
Third	445 B.C.	Nehemiah	Nehemiah	Artaxerxes

Nehemiah

The Master Builder

*I prayed to the God of heaven. And I said to
the king, "If it pleases the king, and if your
servant has found favor in your sight, I ask
that you send me to Judah, to the city of my
fathers' tombs, that I may rebuild it."*
NEHEMIAH 2:4

☙

Most notable quality: Trust in God
Most notable accomplishment: Rebuilt the wall around Jerusalem
Date lived: 450 B.C.
Name: *Nehemiah*, meaning "Yahweh comforts"
Major text: Book of Nehemiah

Bare Bones Background

It has been 13 years since Ezra the priest arrived in Jerusalem and
began to model godliness and uphold the authority of God's Word.
Reforms have begun, but over the years, many people have grown cold
toward following God's law. Some have again begun the practice of marrying pagan women. The country is struggling to fend off threats from
hostile neighbors. Nehemiah, a trusted cupbearer of the Persian king
Artaxerxes, hears distressing news on the state of affairs in Judah. Jerusalem is being held in contempt by its surrounding neighbors because

its walls still lay in ruins, even though many Jews have already returned to this city and their homeland.

Quick Sketch

Nehemiah is ashamed that God's holy city should be held in such contempt. As he begins to pray about this, he develops such a burden for Jerusalem that he asks permission from the king for a leave of absence to go to Judah as its governor with the desire to restore the reputation of Jerusalem.

When Nehemiah arrives, he finds the condition of Jerusalem just as he has been told. He motivates the entire population of the city to start rebuilding the wall, which had been in ruins for 130 years. The feat is completed in just 52 days! Then Nehemiah must deal with hostile neighbors, greedy leaders, and a people who have lost their zeal for God. With the help of Ezra, the priest, the law is taught, and people respond and reforms are again instituted. Nehemiah returns from his leave of absence to the king, but then returns to Jerusalem for a second term as governor and finds that once again the people have drifted away from God. He again insists on and obtains the people's obedience to God's law.

The Big Picture

▶ **Nehemiah's vision is formed**—*Nehemiah 1*

Nehemiah is greatly disturbed when he hears that Jerusalem is in such sad condition. Aware that the cause of the problem lies with the sin of the people, he prays and mourns for days. From his time in prayer he realizes that the people must honor God and rebuild their city walls. As the vision is forming in his mind, he also realizes that as the king's trusted cupbearer, he has the resources to help.

▶ **Nehemiah's vision confirmed**—*Nehemiah 2*

To this point, Nehemiah hasn't committed himself to anything. As a key official to the king of Persia, Nehemiah asks and is granted the authority and materials needed to do his part in the completion of Jerusalem's wall. Now Nehemiah is committed!

▶ Nehemiah shares his vision—*Nehemiah 3*

When Nehemiah arrives in Judah, he shares his vision with the people, who are needed to help complete the wall. The people are motivated as he appeals to their national pride and his confidence in God's support. The people respond and affirm Nehemiah's vision.

▶ Nehemiah's resolve—*Nehemiah 4*

The people surrounding Jerusalem oppose the rebuilding of the wall and plan attacks upon the workers who are building the wall. Refusing to be intimidated, Nehemiah arms the workers, who work and keep watch in shifts.

▶ Nehemiah's example—*Nehemiah 5*

Enemy opposition and difficult times have produced great financial burdens on the people. To survive, many have borrowed money at high rates of interest to buy food. Not being able to repay the loans, the local princes and nobles confiscate the people's homes and land, forcing many to even sell their children into slavery to pay their debts. Nehemiah has set the example by not taking tax money for his own expenses. He now forces the wealthy to restore the lands they have taken and to cancel their loan interest charges, which had been forbidden by the law (Deuteronomy 23:19-20).

▶ Nehemiah's ultimate goal—*Nehemiah 8–10*

Nehemiah's immediate goal is to see the wall rebuilt, but his ultimate goal is to see the people honoring God in their lives. To accomplish this, Nehemiah calls a national assembly so that Ezra the priest can teach the people God's law so they could identify the ways in which they had violated the law. Nehemiah can't bring about revival, but God's Word can. The people respond to the teaching by confessing their sins and agreeing to make corrections in their lifestyles.

The Portrait

From the day that Nehemiah understood his part in God's plan for the people of Judah, his trust in God's provision and protection was unshakable. His confidence was contagious, and the people responded by working together to rebuild the city wall. Nehemiah didn't ask anything of the people that he wasn't living out in his own life. He also provided for his own needs and those of his people, which helped lessen the tax burden on the people. And finally, his personal integrity and compassion served as a model of spiritual leadership for the nobles and rulers who were exploiting the poor people in Jerusalem. His life and practices continue to be an example and a guide for spiritual leaders in the church down through the centuries.

Life Lessons from Nehemiah

Prayer expands your vision. Nehemiah prays for the needs of his beloved Jerusalem. As he prays, he begins to realize that God has put him in a strategic place to provide for that need. Nehemiah's prayers helped to expand his vision of his own usefulness. What burden is on your heart? Allow God to expand your vision as to how that burden can be lifted. Might you be the answer to your own need, or is God's directing your resources elsewhere? In either case, prayer is the starting point for expanding your vision.

Trust God to provide and protect. Nehemiah comes to Jerusalem trusting in God's ability to provide not only for his needs but for those of the people. His confidence in God inspires people to trust in God as well. How strong is your faith in God's provision and protection? Trust God in the midst of your troubles, and your confidence will inspire others to put more trust in God as well.

Teamwork is essential for the completion of major tasks. When Nehemiah arrives in Jerusalem, he observes a city whose walls have been in ruins for more than 100 years. He appeals to the people's national pride and offers his support and that of the Persian king. The people respond by working side-by-side to complete the wall in an amazingly short time—52 days! Do you have a task that seems overwhelming? It probably is, if you are attempting to do it alone. Who can you draft to help? Any task has more chance of completion if you enlist the help of others.

Approximate Time Line for Nehemiah's Service

Prays and receives permission	(5 months)
Travels to Jerusalem	(4 months)
Rebuilds the wall	(52 days)
First term as governor	(12 years)
Returns to Persia	(9 years)
Second term as governor	(14 years)

The events of Nehemiah's life are recorded
by Ezra no later than 400 B.C.

Esther

The Queen

*Yet who knows whether you [Esther] have
come to the kingdom for such a time as this?*
ESTHER 4:14

☖

Most notable quality: Courage and careful planning
Most notable accomplishment: Saved the Jews from extinction
Date lived: Between 538 B.C. to 473 B.C.
Name: *Hadassah* is her Hebrew name, which means "myrtle." *Esther*
means "star" in Persian
Major text: Book of Esther

Bare Bones Background

At this time in history, Persia dominates the entire Near Eastern
world, comprised of 127 provinces stretching from India to Ethiopia.
The winter residence of the king (one of four places) is in a citadel on a
fortified mountain above the city of Shushan. The king has deposed his
queen, and his leaders suggest an empire-wide search for a new queen.
From the beginning of the search until the coronation of the new queen,
four years will go by.

An added drama to all this is the 550-year-old feud that, at this time,
is played out between an Agagite, Haman, and a Benjamite Jew named
Mordecai. In spite of such a lengthy passage of time, neither Haman nor
Mordecai have forgotten that King Saul, a Benjamite, had been ordered
by God to kill all the Amalekites, along with their king, Agag.

Quick Sketch

As the orphaned daughter of Abihail, Esther grows up in Persia with her older cousin, Mordecai, who raises her as if she were his own daughter. Esther is exceptionally beautiful and is chosen to replace the deposed queen. Esther's life in the palace chronicles how actively the forces of evil are trying to eliminate the Jewish race, and her story reveals how faithfully God sovereignly preserves His people. Esther's influence with the king saves the day for the Jews. When the crisis of their near extinction is over, the Jews institute the two-day festival of Purim (meaning "lot"—3:7; 9:26), which becomes an annual observance to celebrate their survival.

Esther is never heard of again, but some historians suggest that she was the stepmother of Artaxerxes. She could have influenced him to look favorably upon the Jews, especially Nehemiah, his cupbearer, and Nehemiah's desire to rebuild the wall around Jerusalem.

The Big Picture

▸ The former queen's banishment—*Esther 1*

After a succession of banquets, Vashti, the queen, is asked to "show her beauty" (verse 11) to the drunken officials present. In her modesty, she refused, causing the enraged king to depose Vashti.

▸ Esther's opportunity—*Esther 2*

After an empire-wide search, Esther is chosen as one of the finalists to become the next queen. She quickly gains the favor of the chief eunuch, who gives her preferential treatment in preparation for her time with King Ahasuerus, also know as Xerxes. The king falls in love with Esther and makes her queen. All this time, Mordecai is performing official duties at the king's gate. He hears of a plot to kill the king and passes this information on to Esther, who, in turn, passes the details on to the king in Mordecai's name.

▸ Esther's doom is secured—*Esther 3*

After Esther becomes queen, her cousin, Mordecai, refuses to bow before Haman, who has become the prime minister and second in command of the country. This so infuriates Haman that he resolves not only to put Mordecai to death, but also to slaughter Mordecai's entire people (this would exact revenge on the Jewish race for its actions toward his ancestors). Haman secures the king's permission to do this, and sets a date.

► Esther's responsibility—*Esther 4*

When Mordecai learns of Haman's plot, he rushes to the palace to inform Esther, weeping and mourning all the while. At this point Esther's reaction is one of helplessness. She cannot approach the king without being summoned, on pain of death. But at Mordecai's insistent prodding, she resolves to do what she can to save her people. She asks that all the Jews in the city pray and fast in preparation for her visit to the king.

► Esther's party—*Esther 5*

Esther appears unsummoned before the king, who not only does not kill her, but promises to grant her anything she requests. Esther asks the king to a dinner party, and invites Haman. At the dinner party, the king again asks what he can grant to Esther. Esther asks that the king and Haman come back for a second banquet. While Haman waits for the second party to take place, he has a gallows made for Mordecai, who is to be hanged on the next day.

► Esther's cousin is honored—*Esther 6*

During the night before the second banquet, the king, in a fit of sleeplessness, asks that the official records be read to him. He is reminded that he has never honored Mordecai for a plot on his life. The next morning, the king asks Haman how he could give honor to a deserving individual. Haman makes a suggestion, thinking he is the one to be honored. To Haman's horror, he is required to lead Mordecai on a horse around the city square, all the while proclaiming Mordecai's honor.

► Esther's people are saved—*Esther 7–9*

At the second party, the king again asks what he can do for Esther. She tells of Haman's plot against the Jewish people, and reveals her identity as a Jew. The king responds to her plea for help by having Haman hanged on his own gallows and giving the Jews permission to defend themselves on the day they were to be exterminated, which they do with great success.

▶ **Esther's cousin is promoted**—*Esther 10*

Esther's story ends with Mordecai's elevation to the office of prime minister, the post vacated by Haman. Together, Esther and Mordecai are a powerful force for the protection of the Jews throughout the Persian Empire.

The Portrait

Esther's external beauty was the vehicle God used to bring her into a place of influence. But there was much more to Esther than her beauty. She seemed to also possess a natural grace and dignity that procured the favor of all those within the palace. And even after she was in the powerful place of queen, Esther continued to appreciate and heed the advice of her older cousin, Mordecai. But her most sterling quality was her willingness to sacrifice her life to preserve the destiny of the Jewish nation. Her courage was evident in her statement, "I will go to the king, which is against the law; and if I perish, I perish!" (4:16).

Life Lessons from Esther

God has a purpose for your present situation. At a critical point in the drama unfolding in the palace, Mordecai reminds Esther that she is involved in a much bigger issue than just her own preservation. God has placed her in a unique situation, with plans to use her beauty, her nationality, and her influence to save an entire race! God has fashioned you exactly as you are and has placed you in a unique place, too—just like Esther—to be used to accomplish His work. Your assignment may not be as big as saving a nation of people, but whatever it is, it has been tailor-made just for you. Step out in courage as Esther did, and accept the challenge of God's purpose for your unique place in life.

Serving God may require that you move out of your comfort zone. Even though Esther is the queen, her life is never secure, especially as she risks her life coming before the king. What if God asks you to step outside your "safe zone"? Like Esther, you have a choice. You can stay where you are and be secure. Or, as in Esther's case, moving in God's direction may involve risking your security. God has a purpose for you, and that is to serve Him. Ask God to give you the courage to step outside your comfort zone and take some risks, for Him, always being assured of His presence.

God's protective hand is always there, even though it is not always visible. Nowhere in the record of the life of Esther is God's name mentioned, but His providential hand is seen in her every move. God is at work in your life too, whether you realize it or not. Ask Him to give you eyes of faith to see His fingerprints on your every situation. Knowing He is present though unseen should give you great comfort as you face the issues of life.

Esther's Possible Influence on Behalf of Returning Jews

- First Jews leave Persia in 538 B.C. with King Cyrus' blessing.

- Esther and Mordecai give the Jews empire-wide credibility during Ahasuerus's reign (483 B.C. to 465 B.C.).

- Esther is stepmother of Artaxerxes, who allows Ezra to lead Jews to Jerusalem and take along large amounts of gold for the soon-to-be-rebuilt temple (458 B.C.).

- Esther continues her influence on her stepson, Artaxerxes, who gives large amounts of supplies to Nehemiah so he can rebuild the walls around Jerusalem.

Isaiah

A Willing Servant

I heard the voice of the Lord, saying:
"Whom shall I send, and who will go for
Us?" Then I said, "Here am I! Send me."
And He said, "Go, and tell this people..."
ISAIAH 6:8-9

Most notable quality: Boldness
Most notable accomplishment: Wrote the great Old Testament book bearing his name
Date lived: Ministered for more than 50 years (739 B.C. to 686 B.C.)
Name: *Isaiah*, meaning "the Lord is salvation"
Major text: Book of Isaiah

Bare Bones Background

Isaiah is a prophet who ministers to the people in and around Jerusalem in the southern kingdom of Judah. His prophetic ministry spans 53 years, including the reigns of four kings: Uzziah, Jotham, Ahaz, and Hezekiah and is recorded in the book that bears his name, Isaiah. During the early years of Isaiah's ministry, the northern kingdom is taken into captivity by the Assyrians (722 B.C.). Assyria's intimidation of the tiny nation of Judah will continue until the reign of Hezekiah, when God miraculously wipes out the entire Assyrian army in one night as it attempts to capture Jerusalem (701 B.C.). The prophets Hosea and Micah are Isaiah's contemporaries. Hosea preaches to the northern kingdom, and Micah and Isaiah minister in the south.

Quick Sketch

Even though Isaiah has a long and fruitful public ministry, little is known about his private life. We do know Isaiah's father was Amoz. Isaiah's family must have had some stature because he has access to King Ahaz and is aware of the political conditions of the region. He is married and has two sons, and when he is called into the prophetic ministry, he eagerly responds with "Here am I! Send me" (6:8). But sadly, he is told that many people won't respond to his preaching. Unlike other writing prophets, Isaiah displays little emotion in his book. He lives to record the death of Sennacherib in 681 B.C. Tradition has it that Isaiah met his death at the hand of the wicked King Manasseh, who had the prophet sawn in two (Hebrews 11:37).

The Big Picture

▶ **Isaiah's ministry during the time of Uzziah**—*2 Kings 15:1-7; Isaiah 6:1*

Isaiah begans his public ministry during the prosperous 52-year reign of Uzziah, also know as Azariah. The spiritual condition of the country begins to decline, and Uzziah's downfall results from his attempt to assume the role of a priest and burn incense on the altar. God afflicts Uzziah with leprosy, from which he never recovers. During the year of Uzziah's death, Isaiah is given a vision of God's majestic holiness (Isaiah 6:1-7), and he receives his call to prophetic ministry:

> I saw the Lord sitting on a throne, high and lifted up, and the train of His robe filled the temple...
>
> Also I heard the voice of the Lord, saying: "Whom shall I send, and who will go for Us?" Then I said, "Here am I! Send me." And He said, "Go, and tell this people..." (verses 1,8-9).

▶ Isaiah's ministry during the time of Jotham—*Isaiah 1–5*

After the death of Uzziah, Uzziah's son Jotham begins a 16-year reign. Isaiah receives the prophecies contained in the first five chapters of Isaiah during Uzziah's reign, and the spiritual condition of the people does not improve during Jotham's reign. A great amount of spiritual corruption still exists in the land.

▶ Isaiah's ministry during the time of Ahaz—*2 Chronicles 28*

Isaiah receives and records much of the prophetic material found in Isaiah 7–27 during the 16 years of Ahaz's reign. Ahaz is a wicked and idolatrous king, and God delivers him into the hand of Syria and Israel. Isaiah warns against political involvement with surrounding nations, but unfortunately, Ahaz will not listen. Instead of asking for God's help against the attacks by Israel and Syria, Ahaz turns to the Assyrian king for assistance. The alliance with Assyria leads to the placement of a heathen altar in Solomon's temple (2 Kings 16:10-16). During this period Isaiah predicts judgment on Israel and Syria, as well as on other surrounding nations, such as Egypt, Moab, and Edom.

▶ Isaiah's ministry during the time of Hezekiah—*Isaiah 36–39*

Hezekiah reigns for 29 years and is one of the few kings in the south of whom it was said, "He did what was right in the sight of the LORD, according to all that his father David had done" (2 Kings 18:3). Isaiah's account of Hezekiah's reign is found in chapters 36–39 of Isaiah. The Assyrian threat continues to escalate, and Hezekiah's advisors want the king to seek an alliance with Egypt. Isaiah gives a lengthy warning against forming alliances with Egypt (Isaiah 28–35), and Hezekiah listens, and puts his trust in God. As a result of the preaching of Isaiah and the prophet Micah and the leadership of godly king Hezekiah, the Assyrian threat is averted, and a significant spiritual revival occurs.

The Portrait

Isaiah directed the major thrust of his ministry to the southern kingdom of Judah. He condemned the empty ritualism of his day and the idolatry into which so many of God's people had fallen. He predicted the coming Babylonian captivity of Judah because of her sin of idolatry.

More than any other Old Testament prophet, Isaiah furnished data on the future day of the Lord and the time following. He described many aspects of Israel's future kingdom on earth—details that are not found in other scriptures. Isaiah is also know as the "evangelical prophet" because of his focus—especially in the last 27 chapters of his book—on the grace of God not only toward a repentant Israel, but also toward all others who repent of their sin.

Life Lessons from Isaiah

Service to God doesn't require public notice. Isaiah was a great man with a prominent ministry, yet little is know of his life. His motivation for ministry wasn't driven by a need for public distinction or to be the center of attention. What are your motives in your service to God? If they are for anything other than the glory of God, they are misdirected. Seek to serve God and His people without demanding the public spotlight. Service to God in any capacity is reward enough.

A righteous God requires a righteous response. Isaiah's vision of the holiness of God made him humbly aware of the judgment he deserved for his own sinful condition. He realized that before he could be used, he would need his life purified. A sense of unworthiness should be your response every time you come into the presence of a holy God through prayer. Like Isaiah, you must see your life in the light of God's holiness. And like Isaiah, you need the purifying work of God's Spirit in your life—no matter how painful that might be—so as to prepare you, like Isaiah, to be mightily used of God.

God's message must be faithfully communicated in spite of the response. God did not promise Isaiah great success when He commissioned him for ministry. Yet Isaiah eagerly responded to God's call. Kings ignored Isaiah's warnings, and the government accused him of treason because he disapproved of its actions apart from the blessings of God. Yet for more than 50 years Isaiah faithfully proclaimed God's message anyway. Today, God is calling you to take His message to your family, friends, and workmates. Will you, like Isaiah, eagerly accept the call? God is asking you to faithfully communicate the message of Jesus Christ, and patiently leave the response in His hands.

Isaiah's Prophetic Ministry
100 Percent Accurate Fulfillment

- Isaiah predicted that the Assyrians would not capture Jerusalem, even though they had defeated all the other countries in their path.
- Isaiah predicted Hezekiah's recovery from a critical illness.
- Isaiah named Cyrus king of Persia as Judah's deliverer from Babylonian captivity 150 years before Cyrus became king.
- Isaiah predicted many aspects of Christ's first coming. All these prophecies were fulfilled 700 years later.

Jeremiah
The Weeping Prophet

*"Ah, Lord GOD! Behold, I cannot speak, for I am
a youth." But the LORD said to me: "Do not say,
'I am a youth,' for you shall go to all to whom
I send you, and whatever I command you, you
shall speak. Do not be afraid of their faces, for
I am with you to deliver you," says the LORD.*
JEREMIAH 1:6-8

☧

Most notable quality: Endurance
Most notable accomplishment: Author of Jeremiah and
Lamentations
Date lived: 646 B.C. to 561 B.C. (85 years)
Name: *Jeremiah*, meaning "Jehovah appoints or sends"
Major text: Book of Jeremiah

Bare Bones Background

The age of Assyrian dominance is over, and the new world power
is Babylon. The Babylonians have overwhelmed Assyria, then Egypt,
and now surround the tiny nation of Judah. The spiritual condition of
Judah is one of flagrant idol worship. Jeremiah is called to preach God's
message of impending judgment during the reigns of the last five kings
of Judah, a period of 40 years, from 627 B.C. to 586 B.C. Sinful Judah is
unwilling to repent, and God will use the Babylonians as His instrument of

judgment. Among Jeremiah's contemporaries are the prophets Habakkuk, Zephaniah, and Ezekiel.

Quick Sketch

During the reign of Manasseh, Judah's most wicked king, Jeremiah is born in the small village of Anathoth, three miles northeast of Jerusalem. Jeremiah is the son of a priest named Hilkiah, and remains unmarried his entire life. After his call into prophetic ministry, Jeremiah is assisted by a man named Baruch, who is responsible for copying down and protecting the prophet's messages. For 40 years, Jeremiah appeals to his countrymen to repent and avoid God's judgment at the hands of an invading army. There is a brief period of reformation during the time of King Josiah (640 B.C. to 609 B.C.), but after Josiah's death, Judah returns to her old ways and refuses to repent, and invasion becomes certain. Jeremiah then pleads with the nation not to resist the Babylonian invasion, which will lead to total destruction. Jeremiah even predicts the length of Judah's exile in captivity—70 years (25:11). Again, the people will not listen.

After the fall of Jerusalem in 586 B.C., Jeremiah is forced to go with a fleeing remnant to Egypt. Tradition claims that when Egypt is invaded by Babylon, Jeremiah is taken to Babylon, where he has the opportunity to write his sad funeral dirge, Lamentations, and to finish his book, Jeremiah.

The Big Picture

▶ **Jeremiah's call**—*Jeremiah 1:5-19*

God gives Jeremiah the priest numerous messages over a period of 40 years. The first of these messages has to do with his call to prophetic ministry. God informs Jeremiah that he was set apart for service before he was born. His special purpose is to take an unpopular message of judgment to the people of Judah. God assured Jeremiah that even though the people would resist his warnings, no one would be able to prevail against him (verse 19).

▶ **Jeremiah's neighbors**—*Jeremiah 11:18-23*

Jeremiah is unpopular and hated by all, even in his hometown of Anathoth. To his sorrow, God reveals to him that his neighbors in Anathoth are plotting to kill him because of his preaching against idolatry. Deeply shaken, Jeremiah asks God to judge these people for their unbelief. God assures Jeremiah that the citizens of Anathoth will be dealt with in the coming Babylonian invasion.

▶ **Jeremiah's dejection**—*Jeremiah 15:15-21*

Jeremiah's emotions surface as he feels the intense antagonism and unrepentant spirit of the people of Judah. In a moment of self-pity, Jeremiah wishes he had never been born. God reassures Jeremiah of His divine protection. Jeremiah again reminds God of his faithfulness, his love, and his separation from evil as one standing alone. Then, even though God has already given Jeremiah assurance, the prophet asks that God not fail him. God reprimands Jeremiah for his self-pity and tells him to repent and regain his focus as God's spokesman.

▶ **Jeremiah's personal life**—*Jeremiah 16*

Jeremiah is told not to marry and have a family because of the terrible future that is in store for Judah. He is told not to mourn the deaths of friends. He is not to take part in any feasting. He is to spend his life speaking words of condemnation on the sins of the people. He is to let the people know that their generation will only see death. It is not surprising that the people who hear these words shun Jeremiah and leave him isolated and alone.

▶ **Jeremiah's confidence**—*Jeremiah 20*

Jeremiah's feelings often waver between wanting to quit (verse 9), being encouraged (verses 9,11), asking for help (verse 12), praising God (verse 13), and succumbing to depression (verses 14-18). In the face of all the hatred, ridicule, persecution, and threats of death aimed at Jeremiah, only the prophet's relationship with the Lord sustains him, giving him confidence and helping him to keep his heart and mind focused on the Lord.

▶ **Jeremiah's hope**—*Jeremiah 31*

Not all Jeremiah's prophecies have to do with judgment upon Judah.

He also gives hope with his prophecy of the new covenant with Israel. God promises that one day, He would make a covenant with Israel—not like the one written on stone (the Ten Commandments), but one written on their hearts by the Spirit of God (Jeremiah 31:31-34).

The Portrait

Jeremiah lived during a time of apostasy in Judah. His nation had abandoned God and was deeply resentful of Jeremiah's repeated warnings of coming judgment because of their sins. Enduring their hostilities, Jeremiah faithfully proclaimed God's words of warning for 40 years. He was totally rejected by his neighbors and countrymen.

Alone most of his life, Jeremiah was forced to turn to the Lord, to whom he poured out his heart, expressing anger over the people's rejection of God's warnings, grieving over the coming judgment, and agonizing over the sight of Jerusalem's destruction. God continually encouraged Jeremiah, but would not let the prophet retreat from his uncomfortable ministry. His great sorrow for the people earned Jeremiah the title of "the weeping prophet."

Life Lessons from Jeremiah

Feelings of inadequacy are no excuse for failing to respond to God's call. Jeremiah thought he was too young and inexperienced to be used by God. But God promised to be with him and to give him the words that needed to be said. You must never allow feelings of inadequacy to keep you from following God's call to serve. If God has a job for you, He will provide the resources for you to carry it out.

Difficulties are unavoidable, but God promises to see you through them. Jeremiah's life was filled with adversity. He was ignored and hated. His life was threatened on many occasions. He suffered continual persecution. Yet by depending on God's love, he endured. You may never have to face the level of persecution experienced by Jeremiah, but you can still draw on the same resources God made available to Jeremiah. Don't focus your thoughts, prayers, and energy on getting out of difficulties. Instead, draw on God's resources to see you through them.

Your heart should beat with compassion. Jeremiah was told by God to preach a message of judgment. This assignment was painful enough, but then Jeremiah was also forced to observe the suffering of his nation because of the people's lack of obedience to that message. He was heartbroken as he saw their rejection and their resultant suffering. How often is your heart broken over the rejection of your lost family members, friends, and neighbors? Ask God to give you a broken heart like that of Jeremiah so you will feel more deeply the need to share God's call to repentance.

Jeremiah's Life of Persecution
Death threats (11:18-23)

Isolation (15:15-21)

Whippings and the stocks (20:1-2)

Narrow escapes from death (26:7-24)

Imprisonment (37:15)

Starvation in a cistern (38:6)

Abduction (43:6)

Ezekiel
The Street Preacher

*Son of man, I have made you a watchman for
the house of Israel; therefore hear a word from
My mouth, and give them warning from Me.*
EZEKIEL 3:17

⚛

Most notable quality: Faithfulness no matter what
Most notable accomplishment: Proclaims prophecies of
Israel's future restoration
Date lived: 623 B.C. to 571 B.C. (lived 52 years)
Name: *Ezekiel*, meaning "strengthened by God"
Major text: Book of Ezekiel

Bare Bones Background

The Babylonian Empire is firmly in control of the entire region from
Egypt to the Persian Gulf, having conquered all opposing forces. In 605
B.C., Babylon begins the systematic deportation, over a period of years,
of three groups of Jews back to Babylon. A young teen by the name of
Daniel is in the first group, which is composed of educated and gifted
children of royal and noble birth. This deportation marks the beginning of the predicted 70 years of exile for Judah (Jeremiah 25:11). The
next group of 10,000 to be taken into exile includes a 25-year old priest
named Ezekiel. After he and his wife are settled in Tell-Abib, on the
bank of the Chebar River, Ezekiel begins a 22-year career as a "street
preacher" among the exiles. His initial message deals with the imminent

and complete destruction of Jerusalem and Solomon's temple. When the destruction comes, the third and final deportation, occurs with few remaining survivors left in the land.

Quick Sketch

In dramatic fashion, Ezekiel is given a glorious vision of God and His throne in heaven. This blazing vision of God's glory and power will strengthen Ezekiel for the difficult ministry that is to come. Many of the Jewish exiles in Babylon are hoping they will soon be able to return to Judah, so at age 30, Ezekiel is commissioned by God to proclaim the impending destruction of Jerusalem unless its inhabitants repent. Then when Jerusalem is destroyed, Ezekiel brings a message of hope to the discouraged exiles—a hope for the future, when God will restore the people of Israel to their homeland and shower blessings upon them during the coming kingdom reign of the Messiah, Jesus Christ.

The Big Picture

▶ **Ezekiel's message of destruction**—*Ezekiel 1–33*

Immediately after Ezekiel has his vision of God and His glorious throne, the prophet begins to preach and demonstrate God's truth, and predict the approaching siege and destruction of Jerusalem. The people, who are captive in Babylon, stubbornly refuse to believe that God would destroy His city and Solomon's temple. They expect to return to Judah in the near future. But Ezekiel warns them that punishment is certain because of their sin, and that God will use the heathen Babylonians as an instrument to purify His people. Ezekiel's message of destruction extends to the nations surrounding Judah as well. They dare to mock God by stating that Judah's destruction is the result of God's inability to protect her. These nations too will experience the wrath of God and learn that He alone is powerful.

▶ **Ezekiel's Message of Restoration**—*Ezekiel 33–48*

After the fall of Jerusalem, Ezekiel's preaching goes in a new direction. Now he proclaims the hope of restoration. Jerusalem, the temple, and the people had become defiled, and the cleansing process would require 70 years of captivity. In addition, God promises to restore Israel not only physically to the land, but also spiritually. How would this be done? God would give the people a "new heart" and put His Spirit in them (36:25-27). Ezekiel concludes his prophetic ministry by giving a detailed description of the future temple that will be the focal point of all activity during the coming earthly reign of the Messiah.

The Portrait

From the beginning of Ezekiel's ministry, God described Ezekiel as His watchman on the walls of the city. A watchman has a great responsibility. He is to exercise great vigilance—for if he fails at his post, the entire city he seeks to protect could be destroyed. As a spiritual watchman, it was Ezekiel's job to warn the people of coming judgment. Whereas the prophets Isaiah and Jeremiah gave national warnings, God commissioned Ezekiel to communicate a message of individual obligation. Each person in Judah and each exile in Babylon was responsible to trust and obey God regardless of the responses of others around them.

Ezekiel used visions, prophecies, parables, signs, and symbols as he walked the streets proclaiming and dramatizing God's message to His exiled people. Ezekiel died in Babylon 40 years before his prophecies were partially fulfilled by a first group of Jews who returned to Judah under the leadership of Zerubbabel, a descendant of King David.

Life Lessons from Ezekiel

God is calling you to be His watchman. God called Ezekiel to warn the people of coming judgment if they continued in their sin. If they turned to God, they would be spared. God would hold Ezekiel responsible for his fellow Jews if he failed to warn them of the consequences of their sin. Today, God is calling you to be His watchman. You have a responsibility to warn your family, friends, and workmates of the consequences of living apart from God. How they respond is between themselves and God. Are you ready to assume your watchman's role?

God expects personal obedience. The importance of each person's accountability before God was a central part of Ezekiel's message. God's love and concern for personal holiness extended to each person in Judah and the exiles in Babylon. Today it is easy to think you can blend into the crowd of churchgoers and not feel the weight of personal accountability for your actions before a holy God. But you only have to read Ezekiel's warnings to Judah to realize that God is personally interested in you and your actions. He desires that you "present your [body] a living sacrifice, holy, acceptable to God, which is your reasonable service" (Romans 12:1).

God always gives hope even in the darkest hour. Jerusalem was destroyed, and her remaining inhabitants were dispersed to foreign lands. All seemed hopeless. Yet even at the people's darkest hour, Ezekiel brought God's message of a bright hope for the future. Yes, there was immediate suffering because of sin, but God had a plan for Israel's survival. Today, you may be experiencing a dark and bleak period in your life, but don't despair. God has given you the resources in His Son, Jesus, that allow you to bear up and survive even the most intense sorrow and pain. There is help if you will but draw on His strength and power.

Ezekiel illustrates his messages with...

1. **The vine branch**—Judah serves no other purpose than to be burned (15).

2. **An abandoned child**—describes Israel's betrayal of God's love and compassion (16).

3. **The eagle and the cedar**—pictures King Zedekiah's rebellion and the resultant destruction of Jerusalem (17).

4. **The burning furnace**—explains the process God is going to use to purify His people, via the "heat" of the siege of Jerusalem (22:17-22).

5. **The two harlot sisters**—symbolize the spiritual adultery of Israel and Judah (23).

6. **The cooking pot**—portrays the way God will purify Jerusalem (24:1-14).

7. **The shipwreck**—illustrates the judgment that will fall on the city state of Tyre (27).

8. **The wicked shepherds**—signify the irresponsible leaders of Jerusalem and their judgment (34).

9. **The dry bones**—describe the spiritual renewal of the nation of Israel (37).

Daniel
A Man of Convictions

There is a man in your kingdom in whom is the
Spirit of the Holy God. And in the days of your
father, light and understanding and wisdom,
like the wisdom of the gods, were found in him.
DANIEL 5:11

&

Most notable quality: Integrity
Most notable accomplishment: Faithfully served God while faithfully serving three kings in two empires
Date lived: 620 B.C. to 535 B.C. (lived 85 years or more)
Name: *Daniel*, meaning "God is my judge"
Major text: Book of Daniel

Bare Bones Background

Daniel's story begins in 605 B.C., when Babylon conquers Jerusalem and Daniel is taken captive, back to Babylon, along with other promising young people of noble birth. They are to be trained in all the culture and language of the Babylonians, then serve in various government positions. Daniel will live a long life and see the fall of the Babylonian Empire and the rise of the Medo-Persian Empire. He will live to see the decree allowing the Jews to return to Jerusalem after 70 years of exile.

Quick Sketch

Daniel is a teenager when he is brutally abducted from his homeland and forced into a training program designed to prepare him and other young men for service in the Babylonian government. Using his God-given wisdom and personal integrity, Daniel makes the most of the exile and, with God's help, quickly rises to the role of statesman and counselor of kings. He not only interprets the dreams of kings, but he also receives visions from God that describe the successive stages of Gentile world power down through the centuries until the time when Messiah will put down all Gentile dominance and usher in His great and blessed kingdom.

The Big Picture

▶ **Daniel serves Nebuchadnezzar**—*Daniel 1–2*

Daniel's first exposure to the king that destroyed his country comes after he and his three friends graduate from three years of training in the king's school. They are interviewed by King Nebuchadnezzar and display incredible skill and are found to be more capable than all the others who were trained in that school.

Soon after his promotion, Daniel again meets with the king and reveals the meaning of a troubling dream the king had—a dream that no one else could interpret. The king is deeply impressed and affirms Daniel's God with this statement: "Truly your God is the God of gods, the Lord of kings, and a revealer of secrets, since you could reveal this secret" (2:47). Daniel is made ruler of the whole province of Babylon and chief administrator over all the wise men of the country (verse 48).

Daniel's third recorded encounter with the king comes some time later, when he is asked to interpret another dream. This time Daniel warns the king against arrogantly taking credit for what God has done with him and his kingdom. The king ignores the warning and is driven mad for a time, until he recovers his senses and "blessed the Most High and praised and honored Him who lives forever" (4:34).

▶ Daniel serves Belshazzar—*Daniel 5*

After Nebuchadnezzar's death, Daniel's wisdom seems to be ignored for 20 years until the night before Babylon is to fall to the Medo-Persians. King Belshazzar is hosting a banquet in his palace when writing miraculously appears on a wall. The king is urged to call for Daniel to interpret it, which he does—it is a message of doom from God. That night, the city falls to the Medes and Persians.

▶ Daniel serves Darius—*Daniel 6*

Darius, the king of the Medo-Persian Empire, is now in control and reorganizes all the conquered lands into 120 provinces. Daniel is one of three governors who again distinguishes himself and is being considered for promotion as the single ruler under the king. The jealous and greedy leaders who work with the king hate Daniel, and they set a trap to rid themselves of him. They maneuver Darius into ordering Daniel to be thrown into a lions' den because he wouldn't stop praying to the one true God. Again, as in the past, God protects Daniel, and the leaders are killed by the very lions that were expected to devour Daniel.

▶ Daniel serves God by...

- ...refusing to defile himself with King Nebuchadnezzar's food when he was but a teenager.

- ...going to God in prayer and asking Him to reveal the meaning of King Nebuchadnezzar's dream.

- ...publicly giving praise to God for revealing the meaning of the king's dream.

- ...courageously confronting King Nebuchadnezzar for his pride.

- ...faithfully going to prayer despite a royal decree that outlawed prayer to anyone but the king.

- ...humbly asking forgiveness for himself and the people of Israel in anticipation of the nation's soon release from exile.

- ...becoming a mouthpiece to both Jews and Gentiles by declaring God's plans for the future of the world.

The Portrait

Throughout his long life, Daniel remains totally committed to God despite serving in a political capacity in the governments of two completely secular and pagan societies. He is a person of great integrity and faith, whose total honesty and loyalty won him the respect and admiration of powerful pagan rulers. Yet even in his exalted position of trusted advisor, Daniel remains a humble servant whose honesty is a constant irritation to his greedy and power-hungry fellow politicians. His credibility extends beyond the king's palace and into the writings of Ezekiel, a contemporary, who also lives in Babylon. Ezekiel makes mention of Daniel as one of three men who is known for his righteousness and wisdom (Ezekiel 14:14; 28:3). Daniel's prayerful relationship with God enables him to live uncorrupted and be of great influence at the center of two world powers for over 80 years!

Life Lessons from Daniel

A life of commitment begins with prayer. As soon as Daniel heard of King Nebuchadnezzar's demands that his dream be interpreted, Daniel and his friends went to prayer. Prayer was Daniel's practice his entire life. Prayer "was his custom since early days" (Daniel 6:10), so when issues came up, Daniel was prepared to deal with them. What is your habit of prayer? Don't wait until you are in a difficulty to start praying. Start praying so that when difficulties arise, you are ready for them!

A life of commitment requires convictions. Even as a teenager, Daniel had developed convictions about his dietary habits. Rather than eat the choice foods of the king, Daniel and his three friends chose to follow God's dietary laws—even under the threat of death. This early conviction set the course for the next 70-plus years of Daniel's life. Do you have a set of godly convictions? If not, you are setting yourself up for spiritual defeat. Convictions will keep you from giving in to temptations, and they will offer wisdom and stability in times of uncertainty. They are a must for a victorious Christian life!

A life of commitment results in courage. Daniel's courage in the lions' den came from a lifetime committed to trusting God in every aspect of his life. This was the same courage Daniel's three friends exhibited when they were threatened with death in a fiery furnace if they didn't bow down to the king's image (3:17-18). You may not be asked to face a fiery furnace or a literal lions' den, but daily, your faith is challenged. Do you hold so strongly to your faith in God that no matter what happens, you have the courage to do what honors God? Strengthen your faith daily by prayerfully living out your commitments to God, and He will give you the courage to live each day for Him.

Daniel's Heart Attitude
in the Prayer in Daniel 9

Daniel felt the need to pray—he had a burden.

Daniel made preparations to pray—he fasted, he wore sackcloth and ashes.

Daniel came before God with humility of heart—his actions revealed his heart.

Daniel came before God with an adoring heart—his first words are "O Lord, great and awesome God."

Daniel came with a penitent heart—he acknowledged both his sins and the sins of the people.

Jonah
The Unwilling Prophet

*Arise, go to Nineveh, that great city,
and cry out against it; for their
wickedness has come up before Me.*
JONAH 1:2

⚛

Most notable quality: National pride
Most notable accomplishment: Preached to Nineveh
Date lived: Ministered during the reign of Jeroboam II
(793–758 B.C.)
Name: *Jonah*, meaning "dove"
Major text: Book of Jonah

Bare Bones Background

The kingdom of Israel enjoys a time of relative peace and prosperity during the reign of King Jeroboam II (793–753 B.C.). Both Syria and Assyria are weak, allowing Jeroboam II to enlarge the northern kingdom to the boundaries known during the days of David and Solomon. With this expansion has come a renewed sense of national pride and disdain for the surrounding nations. Spiritually, however, the nation continues its downward spiral into ritualism and idolatry. With peace and prosperity has come an acceleration toward total spiritual bankruptcy.

The prophet Amos will travel north from Judah to address Israel's two primary sins: an absence of true worship, and a lack of justice toward the misfortunate. And at the same time, Jonah, a resident of Gath-hepher (near Nazareth, in the northern kingdom), will be called by God to take a message to a rising world power and one of Israel's chief enemies, Assyria, and its capital, Nineveh. Within 50 years, Assyria will destroy the northern kingdom of Israel and take its people captive.

Quick Sketch

Jonah, the son of Amittai, is a native of the northern kingdom. He is asked by God to go to Nineveh, the capital of the Assyrian Empire. Jonah wants nothing to do with God's call and rebels by getting on a boat in the seaport city of Joppa and heading west toward Tarshish, a city in modern Spain, rather than heading east toward Nineveh. (This is the only biblically recorded instance of a prophet refusing God's call!) God eventually gets Jonah's attention, and Jonah finally obeys, goes to Nineveh, and preaches a message of repentance.

The city responds by repenting, and Jonah is unhappy about this. God patiently reasons with His prophet, revealing His love and compassion for a lost people, which stands in contrast to Jonah's callousness.

The Big Picture

▶ Fleeing from God's presence—*Jonah 1*

Jonah is asked by God to take a message of judgment to Nineveh. Rather than risk his reputation by going to Gentiles, especially Israel's enemy the Assyrians, Jonah flees toward Tarshish in a boat. God, however, brings along a storm that prevents Jonah from fulfilling his purpose.

▶ Inside the belly of a great fish—*Jonah 2*

Jonah realizes that the violent storm assailing the ship is from God, and it is his rebellion that is putting the crew of the ship in danger. So Jonah asks to be thrown overboard. A great fish, prepared by God, swallows Jonah. After three days and nights, Jonah finally calls on the Lord, acknowledging His power over his life, and submits to His call.

▶ Spreading the message of judgment—*Jonah 3*

Jonah is given a second chance to take God's message of judgment to Nineveh. He preaches the world's shortest revival sermon, "Yet forty days, and Nineveh shall be overthrown!" (verse 4), to a city that takes Jonah three days to walk around (about 60 miles in circumference). The city of 600,000 people "believed God...from the greatest to the least" (verse 5). The king leads the way by demonstrating his repentance by exchanging his royal robes for clothes of mourning.

▶ **Hoping for destruction**—*Jonah 4*

God's anger is turned away over Nineveh's sin, and Jonah is angry because he wanted God to pour out His divine wrath upon the city. From the very beginning Jonah had clearly understood the gracious character of God, and that's why he had tried to run from his mission. He had received God's mercy, but he didn't want Nineveh to experience that same mercy.

The Portrait

Jonah was a reluctant prophet given a mission that he didn't want to fulfill. He grew up hating the Assyrians and fearing their cruelty. His hatred was so strong that he chose to run away from God rather than obey Him. After being miraculously swallowed by a large fish, Jonah came to his senses and turned to obey God's command. He traveled to Nineveh and preached God's message of judgment. And sure enough, his worst fears came true—most of the people in the city repented! Jonah was angry that God had spared Nineveh. He wanted the city destroyed. Jonah was more concerned about national pride than the lost—especially because they were his nation's enemy.

Life Lessons from Jonah

God responds to the prayers of those who call on Him. God spared the lives of the sailors on the ship to Tarshish when they pleaded for mercy. God spared Jonah when he prayed from inside the fish. God spared Nineveh when the people responded to Jonah's preaching. God's will is that all should come to repentance. Have you called on the God of mercy? If not, don't wait until it's too late and God's mercy turns to judgment.

God gives you many second chances. God overlooked Jonah's rebellion and gave him a second chance to serve Him: "The word of the LORD came to Jonah the second time" (3:1). God continued to show patience when Jonah became angry over Nineveh's repentance. He ministered tenderly to Jonah even when Jonah had a childish fit over the death of a plant while showing little concern for the spiritual needs of Nineveh. God was patient and gave Jonah second chances. How many second chances has He given you? Stop and recount His repeated goodness and mercy in your life.

God loves all the people of the world. In their national and Jewish pride, Jonah and his nation believed they had an exclusive right to the one true God. To them, He was Israel's God and others were righteously excluded. But God used Jonah as an object lesson to show His love and compassion for all His creation—even Israel's enemy, Assyria. The Assyrians sure didn't deserve God's grace and mercy, but that's the nature of God's grace—His unmerited favor. What is your perspective toward a lost world, starting with those who are close and familiar, and extending to those who are far away and strange in customs and appearance? Become a "world Christian" and view others as God views them—with mercy and compassion and a desire to see them come to repentance and a knowledge of His Son, the Lord Jesus Christ.

You cannot hide from God. In his rebellious state, Jonah tried to flee from God's call on his life. It wasn't long before God demonstrated His omnipresence—meaning He is everywhere. God's presence is just as real today as in Jonah's day. Is God calling you to serve Him in some way, and are you attempting to avoid or ignore Him? God may not intervene in your life as dramatically as He did in Jonah's, but rest assured that you cannot flee from God's presence. Don't wait for Him to use drastic measures. Respond now!

A Bare Bones Overview of the Minor Prophets

Prophet	Date Lived	Where Prophesied	Message
Obadiah	840 B.C.	Judah/Edom	Edom's destruction
Joel	835	Southern kingdom	The coming "Day of the Lord"
Jonah	760	Nineveh	Repent or be judged
Amos	755	Northern kingdom	A warning of coming judgment
Hosea	740	Northern kingdom	The faithfulness of God
Micah	730	Southern kingdom	Leaders must stop exploiting the poor
Nahum	660	Southern kingdom	Nineveh's destruction
Zephaniah	625	Southern kingdom	"The Day of the Lord"
Habakkuk	607	Southern kingdom	Why do the wicked go unpunished?
Haggai	520	Judah	Rebuild the temple
Zechariah	515	Jerusalem	The coming of Messiah
Malachi	430	Jerusalem	Stop withholding from God

Mary

A Maidservant of the Lord

Let it be to me according to your word.
LUKE 1:38

Most notable quality: Humility
Most notable accomplishment: Mother of Jesus
Date lived: 20 B.C. until after Jesus' resurrection and the birth of the church
Name: *Mary*, meaning "bitterness"
Major texts: Matthew 1–2; 12:46; Luke 1–2; John 2:1-11; 19:25; Acts 1:14

Bare Bones Background

It has now been over 400 years since the conclusion of the last book of the Old Testament, Malachi, and over 500 years since the last biblical record of a miracle. During this time, the tiny nation of Judea has been subject to numerous foreign powers. Presently, they are dominated by Rome. In the midst of these political struggles, a small number of devout men and women are waiting for the Messiah, the Promised One, the one whom they believe will free them of foreign domination. Mary, a teenage girl from the town of Nazareth, in the northern part of the country, is one of these devout people. In the fullness of God's timing, she is about to experience the greatest miracle since the beginning of man's history.

A Quick Sketch

Mary is a teenage Jewish girl from a small town in an obscure part of the world. She is of the tribe of Judah and the royal line of David. As a virgin, Mary bears Christ in a miraculous way. After Jesus' birth, Mary formally marries Joseph, the man whom she is engaged to, a righteous man also from the line of David. He is a carpenter, and they live humbly in Nazareth. She and Joseph have four sons and several daughters. The sons' names are James, Joses, Judas, and Simon. Whether she tells her other children about her earlier experiences with the angel, the shepherds, the wise men from the East, or her flight to Egypt is not recorded in Scripture. Mary is present when Jesus performs His first miracle by turning water into wine (John 2:1-8). Only brief mention is given of Mary after this. She is last mentioned in Acts 1:14 as a member of a group of believers praying and waiting for the promise of God's Spirit.

The Big Picture

▶ **Mary's selection**—*Luke 1:26-33*

In the summer of 5 B.C., Mary, a daughter of Heli, of the tribe of Judah, is living in Nazareth. She is a young maiden in her teens, betrothed to Joseph, a local carpenter. Scripture gives no further information about her background. Of all the young Jewish women in Judea, why is she selected to give birth to Christ? Her humility, her gentle and quiet spirit, and her piety give some indication. In God's predetermined plan, at just the right time in history, the angel Gabriel comes to Mary with a message from God and announces that she will be the mother of the long-expected Messiah. This will happen by the power of God's Spirit.

▶ **Mary's submission**—*Luke 1:34-38*

What's amazing about the announcement of Mary's selection, is the way Mary receives the news. She is in no way skeptical or hesitant. She only asks an intelligent question of Gabriel—how could she become the mother of Jesus when she was a virgin? Following Gabriel's explanation of how the miracle would happen, Mary, with complete faith and acceptance, says, "Behold the maidservant of the Lord! Let it be to me according to your word" (Luke 1:38).

▶ Mary's salutation—*Luke 1:39-55*

Mary travels south to visit her older relative, Elizabeth, who is also going to have a baby. To Mary's surprise, as she walks into Elizabeth's house, Elizabeth, no doubt guided by the Holy spirit, expresses praise for the child in Mary's womb. Then Mary, with great joy, worships and gives thanks to God for her yet-to-be-born son and her Savior. Her song to the Lord is filled with many Old Testament quotes. This reveals that Mary's heart and mind are saturated with the Word of God. Her song contains repeated similarities with Hannah's prayers in 1 Samuel 1:11; 2:1-10.

▶ Mary's sorrow—*Luke 2:35*

As God in human flesh, from His earliest conscious years, Jesus must have had an inner awareness of who He was, where He came from, and what His mission in the world was to be. This awareness made for a major difference in the mother-child relationship between Mary and Jesus. Several incidents over the years cause Mary to sorrowfully realize that Jesus is not answerable to her in the sense expected in a mother-son relationship:

- When Jesus was left behind in Jerusalem at age 12, He wasn't a dependent child. He said, "Why did you seek Me? Did you not know that I must be about My Father's business?" (Luke 2:49).

- When Jesus was asked to do something about the lack of wine at a wedding, He states to Mary, "Woman, what does your concern have to do with Me? My hour has not yet come" (John 2:4).

- When Jesus was asked about His family while speaking to a crowd, He said, "Who is My mother and who are My brothers?" (Matthew 12:46-50).

Although highly favored and blessed among women, Mary's life is a bitter cup of sorrow which will be full, and which she will be compelled to drink at Jesus' crucifixion. Isaiah describes Jesus as "a Man of sorrows and acquainted with grief" (53:3), and Mary partook of His sorrow.

▶ Mary's salvation—*Acts 1:14*

Nothing in Scripture suggests that Mary herself should be the object of adoration or worship. Mary's life reveals quite the opposite. From the time she utters her famous Magnificat in Luke 1:46-55, describing Jesus as "my Savior," she realizes her own need of a Savior and recognizes the true God as her Savior. Then after the resurrection and ascension of Jesus, Mary identifies herself as a believer in Jesus as she gathers with other believers in the upper room in Acts 1:14.

The Portrait

Mary is viewed in Scripture as a woman of reflection and humility. Having been told what her life was to become by the angel Gabriel, Mary would absorb each new event in her life with solitary interest. Her life would take on the quality of the meaning of her name, "bitterness," for she would have many bitter experiences and, from this time forward, never be the same. Eight days after Jesus' birth, in accord with the law, Mary and Joseph present Jesus in the temple in Jerusalem, which is a few miles from Bethlehem. Simeon had been told by the Holy Spirit that he would see the "Lord's Christ" before he died (Luke 2:26). He took the child and blessed God and then made a prediction about Jesus and then another prediction about Mary's future: "A sword will pierce through your own soul also" (Luke 2:35).

Because Mary became pregnant with Jesus before she married Joseph, her reputation was forever tarnished (John 8:41). Also, her eldest son would forever be misunderstood—even by her—as, at the age 12, He speaks of being about His father's business (Luke 2:49). In addition, Mary's other children did not believe in Jesus—at least, not at first. In fact, they sneered at Him and, on one occasion, concluded that He was mad. They wanted to take Him away from a large gathering where He was speaking (Mark 3:21,31; John 7:3-5). After enduring 30 years of shame and scorn herself, Mary then endured the rejection of her Son's claims, the sorrow of His trial, and finally, the agony of His crucifixion and death. She found it difficult to be there at the cross and watch her Son die, but she couldn't leave Him, either.

The Bible's last mention of Mary is in Acts 1:14. There, we see her in the upper room, along with her sons, who are now believers. They are praying and waiting along with some others for the coming of the Holy Spirit, who would equip them to serve in the church. With all the suffering Mary has endured, this final glimpse of her is a happy one. Her son is alive forevermore, and her life has changed. Jesus was once her child, but now she is His child. She can rest easy and take her place alongside all others who worship Jesus as the Son of God.

Life Lessons from Mary

Respond positively to the will of God—Mary was told that an amazing thing would happen to her. She would have a baby without the help of an earthly father. Her response, even though she didn't understand how this could be, was one of humble submission. How do you respond when you receive bad news or are subjected to unfair treatment? Do you balk or complain? Do as Mary did. Trust our gracious God to know what is best for your life...even though it may seem crazy or unfair. Accept His will and enter into His perfect plan for you. Life may get difficult at times as it did for Mary, but God saw Mary through, and He will do the same for you.

Hide God's Word in your heart—After the angel Gabriel had given Mary the wonderful news about her future, she traveled to see her cousin, Elizabeth, who was also to have a child. Mary's song of praise upon arriving at Elizabeth's house is called Mary's Magnificat because it magnifies the Lord. In that song of praise are at least 15 quotes from the Old Testament—Mary was uttering what was in her heart. What comes out of your heart and mouth these days? Hide God's Word in your heart so that when you open your mouth, the overflow of God Word will come gushing out in praise.

Spend time alone with God—After Jesus' birth and the arrival of the shepherds, who declared how angelic beings had appeared to them while singing praises to God, the writer Luke says, "Mary kept all these things and pondered them in her heart" (Luke 2:19). Mary spent time reflecting on these events in her life. Let Mary's example serve as a reminder of your need to spend time alone with God so you can reflect on what He is doing in your life. How long has it been since you last spent time alone with God? It is in such times of contemplation that you learn to fully appreciate all that God has done, is doing, and will do. Many times it is this kind of solitude that makes the difference between being an ordinary or an extraordinary Christian.

Other Women in the New Testament Named *Mary*

Mary, the mother of James and Joses (Matthew 27:56)

Mary, the mother of James the Less (Mark 15:40)

Mary Magdalene, from whom demons were cast out (Luke 8:2)

Mary of Bethany, the sister of Martha and Lazarus (Luke 10:39)

Mary, the wife of Clopas (John 19:25)

Mary, the mother of John Mark (Acts 12:2)

Mary, who worked hard for the church in Rome (Romans 16:6)

John the Baptist

The Forerunner of Messiah

Assuredly, I say to you, among those
born of women there has not risen one
greater than John the Baptist.
MATTHEW 11:11

Most notable quality: A fearless spokesman for God
Most notable accomplishment: Last and greatest of the Old Testament prophets, a messenger from God announcing the arrival of Jesus
Date lived: 4 B.C. to A.D. 28
Name: *John*, meaning "God is gracious"
Major texts: Matthew 3; 11; Mark 1; 6; Luke 1–3; 7; and John 1–3

Bare Bones Background

It has been over 400 years since Malachi's final prophetic words were spoken about the coming of "Elijah the prophet" (Malachi 4:5). Elijah or an Elijah-like person was to come and announce the arrival of the Messiah (3:1). Now at last, after hundreds of years, this person's birth is announced by an angel to an aging priest by the name of Zacharias. The angel says that Zacharias's barren wife, Elizabeth, would bear a son and his name is to be John. He will prepare the people of Israel for the coming of the Lord.

Quick Sketch

John's parents are both descendants from the priestly line of Aaron. They are advanced in age; therefore, his birth is as miraculous as is the announcement by the angel, Gabriel. This son is to maintain the restrictive lifestyle of a Nazirite. John is filled with the Spirit of God even while still in his mother's womb. His early life can be summed up in one sentence: "So the child grew and became strong in spirit, and was in the deserts till the day of his manifestation to Israel" (Luke 1:80). From the time John began to preach, he went forth in the spirit and power of Elijah.

The Big Picture

▶ **John's ministry**—*John 1*

As an adult, John lives in the wilderness. He wears a camel's hide, a garment much like Elijah's (2 Kings 1:8), and eats locusts and wild honey. He appears near the Jordan River and begins to preach two main sermons: The promised Messiah is about to appear, and his listeners must repent in preparation for the coming One. John is outspoken and confrontational. He is afraid of no one, especially the religious leaders. He calls them a "brood of vipers" (Matthew 3:7). While the religious leaders scoff at him, the common people, like Andrew and his brother, Peter, and James and his brother, John, are drawn to his compelling message.

▶ **John's discovery**—*John 1*

To prepare for the coming Messiah, John asks the people to be baptized and demonstrate their desire to change their ways. When Jesus comes to be baptized, John objects (Matthew 3:13-15), knowing his relative to be a godly person (Mary and Elizabeth are cousins). Jesus insists on identifying Himself with John's message. During the baptism, John sees the Holy Spirit descend on Jesus and hears the voice of God announcing Christ as His beloved Son (verse 17).

Later, John points out Jesus to his disciples as the "Son of God" (verse 34), then a day later as the "Lamb of God" (verse 36). Once Christ appears, John shifts the focus of his preaching to Jesus. Within months, the crowds that have followed John are following Jesus.

▸ **John's Imprisonment**—*Mark 1:14*

As the crowds decrease, John continues his reproof of Herod Antipas, a son of Herod the Great, for his marriage to his brother's wife, along with other assorted sins. Herod casts John into prison. He fears John and his popularity and is unwilling to do anything more than leave him in prison.

▸ **John's Doubts**—*Luke 7:18-24*

Like so many other pious Jews, John is expecting the Messiah to lead Israel back to its past glory and set up an eternal kingdom. From prison, John doesn't hear any reports that this is taking place. He sends two of his disciples to ask Jesus, "Are you the Messiah, or should we look for someone else?" As John's messengers look on, Jesus heals many people of their illnesses and then quotes Isaiah 35:5-6, a passage describing a function of the ministry of the predicated Messiah. The messengers return to John and share with him this positive proof that Jesus is indeed the promised Messiah of the Old Testament.

▸ **John's death**—*Mark 6:14-29*

Herodias, Herod's wife, is embittered against John for his preaching about her sin and determines to have John killed. She takes advantage of a promise made to her by Herod after her daughter delights him and others at a banquet—she asks for John's head on a platter. Herod reluctantly complies and sends an executioner, who beheads John in prison. John's disciples bury the body and go and tell Jesus of John's fate. Later, when Jesus becomes more well-known, Herod imagines that Christ may be John the Baptist, who has come back from the dead to haunt him!

The Portrait

Jesus called John the last and greatest of the prophets—a great tribute coming from the greatest of all people (Luke 7:28). John was an imposing figure of a man. He had a fiery disposition—like Elijah. Yet, his life was characterized by self-denial, humility, and courage. His appearance and lifestyle were so severe that many believed him to be demon-possessed. In his humility, he thought of himself as only a "voice" calling people to prepare for the coming One, whose shoes he wasn't worthy of untying. And when that One came, he directed his disciples to follow Him. For his courage, John was put in prison and finally put to death at the age of 30, having ministered for only about one year.

Life Lessons from John the Baptist

You must be ready to step aside for someone more gifted. John had a very large and devoted following. Yet, when Jesus arrived on the scene, John immediately pointed his disciples to Jesus. From that point on, John's ministry began to decrease. Like John, you too need to recognize others who are more gifted and be willing to step aside. Like John, your motto should be, "He must increase, but I must decrease" (John 3:30).

You have been equipped by God's Spirit for a mission. The angel Gabriel announced John's birth and gave details of his mission. When John grew up, he dedicated his life to fulfilling his mission. You too have been uniquely gifted by God's Spirit for your singular mission. God has given you all the spiritual resources you will need to accomplish His will for your life. Ask God to help you determine what your mission in life is, and how He wants you to carry it out. God's will for you is unique—let Him know your willingness to be used by Him.

Ask God to give you boldness in sharing Christ. John was bold in confronting others about their spiritual condition regardless of the cost to himself personally. You may never be called to confront sin as John did, but you *have* been called to follow his example and boldly point others to Jesus. At times, this may include confronting the issue of sin and being willing to suffer when people respond negatively.

Who was John the Baptist?

"The voice of one crying in the wilderness:
'Prepare the way of the LORD; make straight
in the desert a highway for our God.'"
Isaiah 40:3

"Behold, I will send you Elijah the prophet before
the coming of the great and dreadful day of the LORD."
Malachi 4:5

Jesus' estimation of John the Baptist:

- He is more than a prophet—He is My messenger
- None born of women is greater than he
- His message evokes a strong reaction

Matthew 11:8-12

John's Baptism

Old Testament roots:
Performed as a rite of purification (Leviticus 15:13)

Why was John baptizing?
Preparing repentant people for the coming of Messiah

What did it symbolize?
Cleansing

Where did John baptize?
The Jordan River

How did John baptize?
He immersed the person into the water (John 3:23)

Why was Jesus baptized?
He was identifying Himself with sinners

How is Christian baptism different from John's baptism?
It is an act of obedience whereby a believer symbolically
identifies with Christ in His death, burial, and resurrection

183

Matthew
The Man Who Left Everything

As Jesus passed on from there, He saw
a man named Matthew sitting at the
tax office. And He said to him, "Follow
Me." So he arose and followed Him.
MATTHEW 9:9

⚭

Most notable quality: Humility
Most notable accomplishment: Wrote one of the Gospels
Date lived: A.D. 5 to A.D. 70
Name: *Matthew*, meaning "gift of God"; Hebrew name *Levi* means "joined"
Major texts: Matthew 9:9; 10:3; Mark 2:14; Luke 5:27-29

Bare Bones Background

Since Israel's return from the Babylonian captivity, the nation has been occupied or under the control of numerous foreign powers. At the time of Matthew's birth, Israel is under the control of the Roman Empire. The people speak their local language, Aramaic, the trade language, Greek, and the language of their Roman conquerors, Latin. The Romans control the trade routes between Egypt to the south and Syria to the north. Local Jews who want to do so can buy tax franchises from the Roman government and collect taxes from those who use these trade routes. Most tax collectors charge higher-than-necessary fees and pocket the excess after giving Rome her share. Many of these tax collectors are despicable and unprincipled villains. Among this unsavory lot is a Jew named Levi, also known by his Greek name, Matthew.

Quick Sketch

Very little is know of Matthew, even though he wrote one of the four Gospels. What we do know is that he is Jewish, and that he is the son of Alphaeus (Mark 2:14). He is a tax collector for the Roman government. Probably because of the fact he comes in contact with many different travelers he seems to have acquired a good bit of knowledge about Jesus—His miracles and His claim to be the promised Messiah. Or it's possible Matthew heard Jesus teach His Sermon on the Mount in the region of Galilee, where Matthew was born and lives. Whatever information or association he has with Jesus stirs his Jewish heritage so that when Jesus shows up at his tax booth, Matthew possesses enough information and faith to drop everything and follow Jesus.

Like most of his fellow tax collectors, Matthew is a rich man, as evidenced by his first recorded act as a follower of Jesus—he gives a great banquet to introduce his friends to Jesus. He then becomes one of Jesus' 12 ambassadors. Tradition says he was burned at the stake having given his all to follow Christ.

The Big Picture

▶ Matthew's Heritage

Matthew's Jewish name, Levi, indicates his lineage in the priestly line of his great ancestor, Levi, one of the sons of Jacob, the father of the 12 tribes. The tribe of Levi was set apart for the worship and service of God, which indicates that Levi has been given a good education and a proper understanding of the Old Testament Scriptures. (This can be seen in his Gospel account of the life of Jesus, in which he often quotes from the Old Testament.)

▶ Matthew's Ministry

From the first days of his conversion, Matthew demonstrates a zeal to introduce others to his Savior. His next recorded act in Scripture is to hold an evangelistic banquet in his home for all his fellow outcasts of Jewish society. Here are some facts about Matthew's evangelistic dinner:

- The dinner is a great feast (Luke 5:29).

- A great many tax collectors and sinners are invited (verse 29).

- Jesus and His many disciples are invited (verses 29-30).

- The religious leaders are critical of Jesus' presence (verse 31).

- Jesus responds, "I have not come to call the righteous, but sinners, to repentance" (verse 32).

Matthew never ceases to have a burden for his people and ministers to Jews both in Israel and abroad for many years. About 30 years after Jesus' death and resurrection, Matthew writes his account of the life and times of Jesus for the benefit of his Jewish audience. In his account he mentions many Old Testament prophecies that affirm Jesus' claim to be the Messiah predicted in the Old Testament.

▶ Matthew's Writing

Trained to properly read and study the law, and gifted with an ability to use a pen, Matthew is used of God to record the life of Jesus in a systematic fashion, relating numerous Old Testament prophecies of the coming of Messiah that are fulfilled in the person of Jesus. Matthew's Gospel account is written at a time when the apostles, as eyewitnesses, are dying or being martyred. Churches are multiplying and a record is needed by the early Christian community as an evangelistic tool for sharing the gospel with the Jewish communities scattered across the Roman Empire.

The Portrait

Matthew was a humble man, even though he was a handpicked disciple of Jesus. In his entire Gospel he spoke of himself only twice: when he recorded his call (Matthew 9:9), and when he listed all 12 disciples (Matthew 10:1-4). He was a student of the Old Testament and quoted out of the law, the Psalms, and the prophets more times than the other

Gospel writers put together—99 times. He was an evangelist whose first act after following Jesus was to call all his friends together to meet Jesus. He had a lifelong burden for his people, and wrote his firsthand account of Jesus' life and ministry for their benefit. His goal was to persuade them that Jesus was the long-awaited Messiah.

Life Lessons from Matthew

Create a natural environment for evangelism. Matthew's first impulse upon following Jesus was to bring his close friends together for a banquet and introduce them to Jesus. Instead of inviting his friends into a religious setting, he brings Jesus into a place where his friends will feel comfortable. If you sense an unbeliever might hesitate to go to church with you, take time to cultivate your relationship with that person and introduce him to Jesus through your life and words in places where he will feel comfortable.

God can use you to make a difference. When Matthew left his secular profession, all he had was his pen and record-keeping skills. Jesus gave him a new use for his skills—keeping a record of what he observed as he followed Jesus. The Gospel that bears Matthew's name is the fruit of his ministry. When you come to Christ, you bring with you a unique set of talents, skills, and experiences. Jesus wants to use you and your unique attributes to make a difference for His kingdom. What you possess can be mightily used of God—so like Matthew, freely give yourself to Jesus to be used as He desires.

No one is beyond the saving grace of God. Matthew is described as "Matthew, the tax collector" in every account of his life. He was an outcast of Jewish society. He was hated and despised by the religious leaders of his day. Matthew's despised life is a reminder to you not to "write anyone off" as a candidate for salvation. Don't shun such people in the same way the religious leaders did. Rather, follow Jesus' example and be a friend of "tax collectors and sinners" (Matthew 11:19).

Following Jesus is costly. Of all Jesus' followers, Matthew had the most to lose. Tax collecting was a lucrative profession. Once he left his job, his financial situation was drastically altered forever. There could be no turning back. Yet Matthew did not hesitate for a moment when Jesus said, "Follow Me" (Matthew 9:9). Have you counted the cost, and are you following Jesus? And don't forget—Jesus isn't asking for just a one-time accounting. He is asking you to count the cost *daily* (Luke 9:23).

Other Tax Collectors Mentioned in the Gospels
(All had positive responses to God)

- The ones hearing John the Baptist's message responded by believing his message and being baptized (Matthew 21:31-32).
- The one in the temple responded, "God be merciful to me a sinner!" (Luke 18:10-14).
- Zacchaeus responded, "Lord, I give half of my goods to the poor; and if I have taken anything from anyone by false accusation, I restore fourfold" (Luke 19:8).

Mark

The Man Given a Second Chance

Get Mark and bring him with you, for
he is useful to me for ministry.
2 TIMOTHY 4:11

☬

Most notable quality: Emphasized Jesus' ministry as a servant
Most notable accomplishment: Became Peter's companion
and wrote the Gospel of Mark
Date lived: A.D. 15 to A.D. 70
Name: John, surnamed Mark
Major texts: Acts 12:12,25; 15:39; Colossians 4:10; 2 Timothy 4:11;
1 Peter 5:13

Bare Bones Background

After the arrest, trial and crucifixion of Jesus, persecution begins to
intensify as the Christian movement grows. The Jewish religious leaders
are intent on stamping out this new religion founded around the life of
Jesus of Nazareth. But persecution didn't slow the growth. Thousands
are coming to Christ. Among them is an influential family with a son
named John Mark. John Mark's mother is very involved with Jesus'
disciples, especially Peter, and conducts prayer meetings in her home.
John Mark moves freely among the disciples and the other members of
the Jewish Christian community.

Quick Sketch

As a teen, Mark may have been an eyewitness of the betrayal and arrest of Jesus in the Garden of Gethsemane. Months after the resurrection, Mark is mentioned in connection with a prayer meeting being held in his mother's home—some Christians had gathered to pray for the release of Peter from prison (Acts 12:12). Mark's cousin, Barnabas, is a leader in the church and becomes an associate of the apostle Paul. Mark is asked to join his cousin and Paul as their assistant on their first missionary journey. For some reason, Mark deserts the team and returns to Jerusalem. Later, when Barnabas wants to take Mark on another missionary trip, Paul refuses, forcing a division between himself and Barnabas. Years later and with a second chance from Barnabas, Mark becomes a useful servant to Paul, and later, to Peter in Rome. It is probably during his time with Peter in Rome that Mark records Peter's account of the life of Jesus in the Gospel that bears his name—the Gospel of Mark.

The Big Picture

▶ Mark's background—*Mark 14:51-52*

Mark is the son of Mary, a prominent and wealthy woman in Jerusalem. There is no mention of Mark's father. Some have suggested that Mary's home is the place where Jesus and His disciples observed the Last Supper. If so, Mark may have been a witness of this impassioned scene, then followed Jesus and His disciples as they went to the Garden of Gethsemane. As the mob approaches Jesus, they also lay hold of Mark. But wearing only a loose linen garment, Mark is able to free himself, leaving behind the garment and fleeing into the night naked.

▶ Mark's family ministry—*Acts 12:12*

Several years after Jesus' resurrection and ascension to heaven, a prayer meeting is held in the home of Mary and her son Mark. The family must have been well acquainted with the disciples and especially Peter, for after his miraculous release from prison, Peter immediately goes to Mary's house to inform the people there that he has been freed.

▶ **Mark's failure**—*Acts 12:25–13:13*

Most likely because of Mark's connections to his mother, Mary, and his cousin, Barnabas, who is now a respected leader in the young church, Mark is asked to travel with Paul and Barnabas on their first missionary journey. He assists the team until it reaches Asia Minor after sailing from Cyprus. For some unknown reason, Mark leaves the team and returns to Jerusalem. His departure doesn't disrupt the team's efforts, but when Barnabas asks Paul to allow Mark to join on the second missionary trip, Paul is adamant in his refusal. Mark can't be counted upon.

▶ **Mark's mentor**—*Acts 15:36–41; 1 Peter 5:13*

Barnabas, whose name means "son of encouragement," lives up to his name as he defends Mark against Paul's concerns about his usefulness. When Barnabas and Paul can't reach an agreement, Barnabas chooses Mark and heads off to Cyprus to minister. Barnabas is an able role model and discipler so that in the years to come, Mark matures and is again seen as useful by the great apostle Paul (2 Timothy 4:11).

▶ **Mark's relationship with Peter**—*1 Peter 5:13*

Peter is familiar with Mark's family—we know this because Peter visited Mark's home after his miraculous release from prison. Peter, in his first letter from Rome, calls Mark "my son." Mark must have been a traveling companion and fellow minister with Peter in Rome, because in this letter, Peter sends greetings from Mark as well.

▶ **Mark's finish**—*Gospel of Mark*

Mark's faithful finish gives encouragement to all who have stumbled along life's rocky way. He typifies all who forge victory from defeat. That he finished well is seen in his authorship of one of the biblical accounts of the life of Jesus. Mark writes from his own brief exposure to Jesus and the disciples and from Peter's firsthand exposure to Jesus and the other disciples. It is not surprising that Mark's account is written for a Roman audience, because it was penned in Rome.

The Portrait

The first two biblical references to Mark show him retreating when faced with outside pressures. The first account depicts Mark running away from Jesus when Jesus was arrested (Mark 14:51-52). The second account describes Mark, assistant to Paul and Barnabas on a missionary team, as "departing from them" and returning to Jerusalem (Acts 13:13). This seems to reveal Mark as being unfit for any significant Christian ministry. Indeed, that's what Paul thought when he refused to take Mark on another missionary trip (15:36-40).

Barnabas, Mark's cousin, saw something redeeming in Mark and separated from Paul and took Mark with him on a different missionary trip. This encouragement from Barnabas paid off in later years, for Mark is mentioned as being with Paul while the latter was in a Roman prison (Colossians 4:10). And when Paul faced execution at the end of his second Roman imprisonment, he asked that Mark come with Timothy to aid him because Mark was "useful...for ministry" (2 Timothy 4:11). Later Mark is mentioned as serving with Peter in Rome (1 Peter 5:13), where Mark may have written his account of the life and ministry of Jesus.

Life Lessons from Mark

Always look for the good in people even when they fail. When Mark departed from Paul and Barnabas, Paul refused to take Mark on the next missionary trip. Barnabas, however, stood by Mark and helped him. In time, Mark came to be a valued worker in Paul's eyes. When you make a spiritual investment in another person, you never know how significant that investment might become, so always look for the best in people. When you treat people as important, they usually respond to your expectations.

Be willing to invest in young people. Mark, a young man, was fortunate in that he had a family member who never gave up on him, but encouraged him and brought him along to maturity. Do you know any young people who need your support in times of difficulty—such as a son, daughter, niece, or nephew? Look first at your immediate family. Then consider the young people in your church. They are the next generation of believers to carry on God's work. Who knows—God may be asking you to disciple and encourage another Mark!

Failure is not the end; it is just the opportunity for a new beginning.

Many who have had a "Mark-like" beginning to their Christian life have gone on to make a significant contribution to the cause of Christ. Have you experienced a "failure" in your Christian life? Learn from your mistake. Ask forgiveness if it is needed, but don't allow a defeat to keep you from serving. Ask God to give you the courage to get up and keep going. It's not how well you start that's important, but how well you finish!

The Twelve Disciples—Bare Bones Description

Peter—An impulsive man, the leader of the disciples (also called Cephas and "the rock")

Andrew—Brought others to Jesus, including his brother Peter

James—Was ambitious, short-tempered, the first disciple to be martyred (one of the Sons of Thunder, along with his brother John)

John—Was known as "the apostle of love" and the disciple Jesus loved (one of the Sons of Thunder, along with his brother James)

Philip—Had a questioning attitude (i.e., asked Jesus how He planned to feed the 5000)

Bartholomew—Doubted the worth of anyone coming from Nazareth (also called Nathanael)

Thomas—Doubted Jesus' resurrection (also called "the twin" and referred to through time as Doubting Thomas)

Matthew—Left his occupation of tax collector to follow Jesus (also called Levi)

James—Son of Alphaeus

Thaddaeus—Asked Jesus if He was going to reveal Himself to the world (also called Judas, the son of James)

Simon the Zealot—Was a fierce patriot of Judiasm (also called Simon the Canaanite)

Judas Iscariot—Was treacherous and greedy, the disciple who betrayed Jesus

Luke

The First Medical Missionary

Luke the beloved physician and Demas greet you.
COLOSSIANS 4:14

Most notable quality: Humble servant
Most notable accomplishment: Wrote more of the New Testament than any other writer
Date lived: Until after A.D. 60
Name: *Luke*, meaning "light"
Major texts: Colossians 4:14; 2 Timothy 4:11; Philemon 24

Bare Bones Background

The world is in transition during the lifetime of Luke, a Greek who grew up in Antioch of Syria. From the time of Alexander the Great, Greek has been the official trade language from Egypt to India. Even under Roman rule, Greek is still spoken and read by most educated citizens. The Greeks valued education, so universities of learning spring up wherever there is a Greek influence. One such university is the great school at Alexandria, Egypt, with its center for medical education and research. Another school of learning is at Antioch, where Luke may have received his training. By the time the apostle Paul begins his second missionary journey, he has passed the age of 50, making him an "elder statesman" for those still living at that time in history. Then when you consider his many beatings, his imprisonments, and his ambitious travel schedule, it isn't any wonder how he might have met Dr. Luke. Luke subsequently gives up his medical practice to accompany Paul. He attends to Paul's health and becomes a "beloved" friend (Colossians 4:14) and an accurate historian of both the life and ministry of Jesus and the birth and spread of the gospel.

Quick Sketch

Luke is mentioned by name only three times in the New Testament—all three mentions are by the apostle Paul while he is in prison. Luke appears to have been a Gentile, because Paul, in his writings, does not include him with the other Jews when he gives his greetings (Colossians 4:7-14). Luke is a physician by profession, but nothing is known of where he received his training. He joins Paul's second missionary journey at Troas, a city in the northern part of present-day Turkey. He sails with the team to the northern province of Macedonia (in Greece) and to a city named Philippi. Luke remains behind until he again rejoins Paul's team on Paul's third missionary journey some seven or eight years later. Luke is the constant companion of Paul for the remainder of Paul's life.

Luke is not an eyewitness of the life of Jesus. He gathers the material for his Gospel record from eyewitness accounts as he travels with Paul to Jerusalem and as he stays nearby during Paul's two-year imprisonment in the provincial prison in Caesarea. Luke is with Paul when the latter is shipwrecked on the way to Rome. In Rome, Luke ministers to Paul while they wait for Paul's audience with Caesar, and during this stay, Luke completes his Gospel account. Luke then remains with Paul as the apostle is again imprisoned for the last time. At one point toward the end, Luke is the only one by Paul's side. Tradition tells us Luke died as a martyr some time after Paul's death.

The Big Picture

▶ Luke's background

Luke shows great interest in Antioch in his historical account of the spread of the church, which has led many to speculate that he was born in Antioch and that he may have become a Christian in the church where Paul and Barnabas form part of the leadership team. There is no indication where Luke receives his formal education, but his excellent writing style and his medical training are indicative of a man who is a highly educated Greek.

▶ Luke the medical missionary

Luke joins Paul and is with him at least intermittently until Paul's final imprisonment in Rome. Luke not only attends to Paul's frail health due to his many beatings, stonings, imprisonments, and shipwrecks, but he surely practices medicine at least at times during their journeys together. At times Luke also shares in the call and labors of preaching. Luke becomes the first university-trained medical missionary.

▶ Luke the historian

Luke's training makes him an able and deliberate historian. He is credited with writing more than one-fourth of the New Testament—more than any other writer. Modern research has verified the accuracy of his work.

▶ Luke the evangelist

Luke makes no claims to being an eyewitness of the life of Jesus. Rather, he affirms that the things he recorded were delivered to him by those "who from the beginning were eyewitnesses and ministers of the word" (Luke 1:2). Luke, being a Greek, writes his account to strengthen the faith of Gentiles, especially Greek believers. He also wants to encourage unbelieving Greeks to consider the claims that Jesus Christ is the Perfect Man—the Son of Man who came in sacrificial service to seek and die for sinful men that He might save them.

The Portrait

Paul's use of the word "beloved" to describe Luke tells us much about Luke's character. Luke was a physician who was trained to care for the physical needs of people. In his writings we see his concern for people—especially the poor, women, and the despised of Jewish society (like Zacchaeus the tax collector), and how they respond to Jesus' ministry. We also see his concern in his ministry to the apostle Paul. In spite of the dangers and hardships that occurred in his travels with

Paul, Luke remained close by this aging evangelist and church planter. When younger men were deserting Paul during the difficult days in Rome, Luke was faithfully there by Paul's side.

Life Lessons from Luke

Give God the best you have to offer. Dr. Luke opened his Gospel account of the life of Jesus by stating that he had "done his homework" (see Luke 1:3). His excellent writing style and his comprehensive personal research have given the world an accurate picture of Jesus, His claims of divine origin, and the proofs that substantiate those claims. Are you approaching your service to God in the same way? Are you serving with excellence? However you serve God, no matter what your area of service, you need to give God the best you have to offer.

Sacrifices are required in serving God. Jesus told His disciples that anyone who follows Him must count the cost (Luke 9:23). Dr. Luke was an educated man with a respectable profession, yet he chose to give up everything to serve God by ministering to the apostle Paul. Discipleship is costly. Are you just "dabbling" in your commitment to Jesus? Count the cost and decide along with Dr. Luke that the cost is worth it. And on the other side of that decision, incredible usefulness is awaiting you for the cause of Christ!

Look for opportunities to serve others. Paul was a respected and highly esteemed Christian worker, yet even he needed the personal care of others, such as Luke. Look at others in your local church, even at those who are the most esteemed. Everyone needs help in some way or at some time. Ask God to give you compassionate eyes, a willing heart, and helping hands. Don't withhold yourself. Others need exactly what you have to offer!

. Luke's Unique Account of the Life of Jesus

He recounts the miraculous birth of John the Baptist.

He alone writes of the boyhood of Jesus.

He makes mention of numerous additional women in the life story of Jesus.

He centers more on prayer than the other Gospels.

He gives special attention to the poor.

He includes nine miracles, 13 parables, and a variety of messages and events not found in the other Gospels.

John

The Apostle of Love

*Now there was leaning
on Jesus' bosom one of His
disciples, whom Jesus loved.*
JOHN 13:23

☙

Most notable quality: The apostle of love
Most notable accomplishment: Wrote five New Testament
books
Date lived: A.D. 5–97
Name: *John*, meaning "the Lord is gracious"
Major text: Gospels; 1, 2, 3 John

Bare Bones Background

The birth of Christianity begins in A.D. 32 on the day of Pentecost
with the coming of the Holy Spirit. Lives are dramatically altered and the
power of God's Spirit is released upon Jesus' followers. This ushers in a
religious movement that begins to sweep across the Roman world. John,
the youngest of the 12 apostles, will experience this great new movement
from its beginnings as the Holy Spirit comes from heaven like a mighty
wind and fills the disciples with power, and they boldly begin preaching
the resurrection of Jesus Christ.

Quick Sketch

John is the son of Zebedee and Salome, and the younger brother of James. He and his family live in Galilee, where the men are fishermen on the Sea of Galilee. This family has some connection with Caiaphas the high priest (John 18:15), which implies a position of influence and means. John and his brother are followers of John the Baptist until the latter points them to Jesus. From that point onward they follow Jesus for intermittent periods of time until Jesus selects John and James, along with ten others, to be His disciples. Jesus commissions John and the others to take His message to the world. John will outlive all the other apostles and experience firsthand, along with many other Christians across the Roman Empire, harsh persecution from corrupt and pagan rulers. These evil men fear this mighty force of committed followers of Jesus. As John nears the end of his life, he will also see false doctrines and heresies creep into the church.

John, the last remaining eyewitness of the life and ministry of Jesus, writes his Gospel as a complement to the other three Gospel accounts that have been in circulation for 20 years or more. Much of John's ministry of writing letters of warning during his final years will come from the city of Ephesus, which has become his headquarters.

Because of John's faithful preaching of God's Word, the Roman government banishes him to a barren island in the Aegean Sea off the coast of Ephesus—an island called Patmos. It is on this small deserted isle that John receives a series of visions that lay out the future history of the world. Eventually he is released from Patmos and returns to Ephesus, where his "Revelation of Jesus Christ" begins its circulation, and where he dies after about a year, thus bringing an end to the age of the apostles.

The Big Picture

▶ **John as a disciple**

- He is an early disciple of John the Baptist (John 1:35-39).
- John the Baptist points John to Jesus (John 1:43).

- John follows Jesus back to Galilee and observes Jesus' miracle of changing water into wine (John 2:2).

- John goes with Jesus to Jerusalem, then back to Jesus' headquarters in Galilee. He returns to his fishing business (John 2:13–4:54) but continues to follow Jesus on an intermittent basis.

▶ John as an apostle

- About halfway through the three years of His ministry, Jesus chooses a group of 12 men with whom He will develop close discipling relationships. John, his brother James, and Peter enter into a more intimate relationship with Jesus than the other apostles.

- John is the only disciple who stays near Jesus throughout His trial and crucifixion.

- From the cross, Jesus appoints John to care for His mother, Mary (John 19:25-27).

- John and Peter are the first disciples to view the empty tomb (John 20:1-10).

▶ John as an evangelist

- John and Peter are put into prison for preaching in the temple area.

- John and Peter preach to the Samaritans.

- John is described by Paul as a "pillar" in the Jerusalem church (Galatians 2:9).

- John and the other apostles stay in Jerusalem preaching and teaching the multitude of new believers.

▶ John as an itinerant preacher

- John remains in Jerusalem until the death of Mary, which then releases him to be an itinerant minister.

- John arrives in Ephesus after the death of Paul. Here he writes the three letters bearing his name and plays a major role in fighting the heresies that begin to show up in the church.

- John is arrested and banished to Patmos, where he writes the book of Revelation.

▶ **John as an author**

- John writes more of the New Testament than any other writer, except Luke and Paul.

- John's Gospel is considered the most theological of the four accounts of Jesus' life. He presents the most powerful and direct case for the deity and humanity of Jesus, the Son of God, God in flesh, the Messiah.

- John's three letters describe, from personal experience, what it means to have fellowship with God, and warn that false teachers are denying both the humanity and deity of Jesus, which his own experience has shown to be untrue. He also warns against showing hospitality to these false teachers.

- His "Revelation" writings begin with a commentary on the spiritual condition of each of the seven churches in the areas around Ephesus, then proceed to describe the church's future struggles until final victory is achieved at the second coming of Jesus Christ as King of kings and Lord of lords.

The Portrait

John was probably the youngest of the disciples, and the most brash and youthfully fiery. His testimony in Scripture was not a pretty one. Three incidents in the Bible illustrated his need for Jesus' transforming work in his life:

1. John was selfish—John and the other disciples thought they were in an elite and exclusive club. Someone outside their club was casting

out demons in Jesus' name, and John and the others opposed him. Jesus rebuked John for his possessive spirit toward anyone ministering in Jesus' name regardless of group affiliation (Luke 9:49-50).

2. John was vengeful—John and his brother were mad that a village in Samaria refused hospitality as the disciples were on their way to Jerusalem. They requested that Jesus send down fire and kill everyone in the whole village! It's surprising that so soon after Jesus' earlier rebuke of John that Jesus again had to rebuke John and his brother James for their evil suggestion (Luke 9:51-56).

3. John was ambitious—John and his brother teamed up and asked their mother to go to Jesus and ask Him for positions of power in His coming kingdom. It didn't matter if they had to step on and over their ten fellow disciples to gain these positions. Again, Jesus rebuked them and took the opportunity to teach the disciples about servant leadership (Matthew 20:20-28).

But Jesus' death and the coming of Jesus' Spirit changed all that for John. The book of Acts and John's own writings reveal him to have become a loving, lowly, and patient servant of his Lord. John lived to the age of nearly 100 years old, and his final words, tradition says, were his life's message, "Little children, love one another" (see 1 John 3:18; 4:7).

Life Lessons from John

Your Christian life is a work in progress. John is popularly known as "the apostle of love." But the Gospel accounts of his life don't show much love. John is seen as selfish, hot-tempered, and ambitious. What happened? The cross happened! In the book of Acts and throughout John's writings, you see how Jesus transformed him into a bold, devoted, unselfish, and humble servant. Where are you on Jesus' transformation scale? Jesus wants to transform you into His image, however long that might take. It's not what or who you are today that is as important as what and who you can be when you give your life totally to Him. God is not finished—you are a work in progress.

Your ability to love others is related to your understanding of God's love for you. John was so awestruck by God's unconditional love and acceptance of him that he described himself as the disciple "whom Jesus loved" (John

13:23). When was the last time you thought about Jesus' infinite love for you—a love so great as to die for your sins so that you might live? Have you accepted Jesus' priceless gift of forgiveness and salvation? Once you comprehend just how much Jesus loves you, and you accept His love, then you will be able to love others much more deeply. And along with John, you can become "the disciple whom Jesus loved."

You must learn to balance ambition and humility. In his youth, John had ambitious plans for himself. Jesus repeatedly made it clear that authority in His kingdom was reserved for the humble, not the ambitious. Yet John's ambition compelled him to do whatever was necessary to have a position of authority. Humility, on the other hand, desires to be worthy to be considered for such a position. Are you ambitious? It is not wrong to be ambitious if it is for the right reason—the glory of God. With humble service, which John performed in later years, you will prove yourself worthy of being given authority.

John's Evidence of Jesus' Divine Nature

The witness of John the Baptist (5:32-33)

The witness of Jesus' miracles (5:36)

The witness of the Father (5:37-38)

The witness of Scripture (5:39)

The witness of Jesus Himself (8:14)

The witness of the Holy Spirit (15:26)

The witness of the disciples (15:27)

Peter

A Fisher and Leader of Men

*And [Peter] said to [Jesus], "Lord, I am ready
to go with You, both to prison and to death."*
LUKE 22:33

☽

Most notable quality: Leadership
Most notable accomplishment: First to preach gospel sermons to both Jews and Gentiles.
Date lived: A.D. 5 to A.D. 65
Name: Hebrew name is *Simon*; Greek name is *Peter*, which means "rock"
Major texts: Gospels; Acts 1–11

Bare Bones Background

In all the biblical accounts of the calling and training of Jesus' disciples, the lists and order of the names of the 12 men are almost identical. In all four Gospels, the first name in these lists is always Peter. From the day that Peter met Jesus, he was singled out by Jesus to be a "rock" of strength for the others. He was a natural-born leader and quickly became the spokesman for the whole group. Yet with all his self-confidence and boldness, Peter was teachable. With each rebuke from the Lord for something he says or does, he is teachable and open to correction. The true secret to his greatness as a spiritual leader can be seen in his own growth as he remains sensitive to the leading of his Lord. This is his desire for us as he writes and encourages us to "grow in the grace and knowledge of our Lord and Savior Jesus Christ" (2 Peter 3:18).

Quick Sketch

Simon is the son of Jonah, and a native of Bethsaida in Galilee. He, along with his brother, Andrew, are early disciples of John the Baptist. Andrew is the first to meet Jesus and then brings his brother, Peter, to meet Him. In predictive fashion, Jesus changes Simon's name to *Cephas,* which, in the local dialect, means "rock," while in the Greek, *Cephas* is translated "Peter." Peter's meeting with Jesus does not result in any immediate change in Peter's external behavior. He returns to Galilee and continues his fishing business. Later he is called by Jesus to become one of the 12 disciples.

It is only after Peter's denial of Jesus and his restoration by Jesus that Peter's fiery disposition is redirected as a "rock" to the rest of the disciples. He is now ready to be a true spiritual leader. After Jesus' resurrection and ascension and the arrival of the Holy Spirit, Peter becomes a key leader and a chief spokesman for the newly forming church in Jerusalem. He ministers to the Jewish community in and around Jerusalem for many years.

Later in life, Peter seems to have traveled and ministered to the scattered Jewish communities as well as Gentiles in Asia minor, because his first letter, 1 Peter, is addressed to the believers residing in several provinces of this area. Peter probably arrives in Rome in the late 50s or early 60s A.D. His two letters are written in Rome during the middle 60s with Silas, Paul's missionary traveling companion, and John Mark at his side. Paul is imprisoned in Rome during this time. Peter and Paul are both martyred about the same time by Nero in A.D. 67–68. Tradition states that Peter's death was by crucifixion. Peter's prominence in the formative years of Christianity makes him one of the most significant men of the New Testament.

The Big Picture

▶ Peter the fisherman

Peter begins his life as a fisherman at Bethsaida, a city near the Sea of Galilee. He and his brother Andrew go into partnership with James and John. All four will later become disciples of Jesus. Their business prospers, allowing them to have social connections with the high priest in Jerusalem. Peter is older than the others and becomes the acknowledged leader of their fishing enterprise. He is married (Mark 1:29-31) and later, when he becomes a missionary, his wife accompanies him on his travels (1 Corinthians 9:5). It is while Peter and his other partners are about the business of fishing that Jesus calls them to "follow Me, and I will make you fishers of men" (Matthew 4:19).

▶ Peter the disciple

The close association of Peter, Andrew, James, and John continues as together they are called by Jesus to be His disciples, along with eight others. They will live with Him, and learn by listening to His teaching. Several events in Peter's life as a disciple reveal much of his impetuous nature:

Peter's walk on water—One night in a storm on the Sea of Galilee, Peter's impulsiveness leads him to try to walk on water in order to be near Jesus. He succeeds...until he takes his eyes off Jesus and begins to sink (Matthew 14:28-31).

Peter's confession—When Jesus asks the disciples, "Who do you say that I am?" Peter promptly replies, "You are the Christ, the Son of the living God" (Matthew 16:16). Jesus then says that He would build His church on the "rock" of Peter's solid statement of truth concerning the divinity and authority of Jesus (Matthew 16:18).

Peter's overconfidence—On the night of the Last Supper, Jesus declares that one of the disciples will betray Him. Peter in his usual fleshly and overconfident manner, promptly declares that under no circumstance would he ever deny Jesus. Jesus then predicts that before the morning light, Peter would deny Him three times.

▶ Peter the preacher

After Jesus' resurrection, Peter preaches to a large crowd of Jews gathered in the temple area for one of the major Jewish holidays. Thousands of Jews come to believe in Jesus, and the church is born. Peter preaches a second sermon later, and more thousands believe. The message spreads to Samaria, and Peter and John are sent by the Jerusalem church to confirm the response and witness the coming of the Spirit upon the Samaritans as well. Peter is also the first to present the gospel to Gentiles, or non-Jews (Acts 10–11).

▶ Peter the missionary

Initially, Peter's ministry focuses on the Jewish communities in and around Jerusalem. Later he travels to other places and shares Christ with Jews who are scattered throughout the Roman Empire. At some point Mark joins Peter and writes his Gospel.

The Portrait

A study of the life and character of Peter reveals many noble qualities. His enthusiasm and boldness are traits every Christian should desire. But some of Jesus' sharpest rebukes were aimed at Peter's misdirected enthusiasm. Peter's intense devotion and commitment to Jesus was demonstrated by his willingness to walk on the stormy waters of the Sea of Galilee to be near Jesus and his fearless use of his sword to protect Jesus. But Peter is just as weak as he is bold—as seen in his denial of Jesus before a lowly servant girl, or in his flight from Jesus at His crucifixion. Peter's positive traits of boldness and devotion are inspiring and worthy of emulation. His negative traits—his thoughtless outbursts, his brashness, and his misdirected enthusiasm—should be a warning for us to avoid such behavior. Overall, Peter stands out as a stellar example of allegiance to our Lord and fruitful ministry for Him.

Life Lessons from Peter

Failure does not disqualify you from serving Jesus. Jesus predicted Peter's failure, then later said, "When you have returned to Me, strengthen your brethren" (Luke 22:32). After each of his failures, Peter always returned with a desire to continue to follow Christ. Jesus knows that no one is perfect—failure is inherent in our humanness. Just as Jesus was ready to forgive and reinstate Peter for usefulness, He is ready to do the same for you. Whatever spiritual failure you are presently experiencing, is an opportunity for you to experience the grace of God. It is better to be a follower who sometimes fails than one who fails to follow.

Spiritual warfare should not be taken lightly. When Jesus warned of coming persecution, Peter was quick to assert he would remain faithful to Jesus. In his overconfidence he believed he could remain strong even when Satan applied spiritual pressure on him. Jesus knew Peter couldn't remain faithful on his own, and predicted Peter's restoration (Luke 22:32). Peter's fall is a reminder that no one is immune to temptations or failure. None of us can stand in our own strength. Jesus said, "Without Me you can do nothing" (John 15:5), which includes withstanding temptation. Always be ready with "the whole armor of God, that you may be able to withstand in the evil day" (Ephesians 6:13).

Evangelism is simply introducing people to the Savior and letting Him do the rest. Peter's brother Andrew doesn't stand out as a giant in church history. Andrew's major accomplishment was bringing Peter to Christ and allowing Jesus to transform Peter into one of the great spiritual leaders of the early church. You may think you don't have much to offer your Savior, but one very important thing you can do is introduce your family, friends, and workmates to Jesus and allow His Spirit to do the rest. Some of the greatest contributors to the cause of Christ down through the centuries have been those who simply introduced someone else to the Savior.

The Contents and Results of Peter's First Sermon

Jesus is a real person (Acts 2:22)

Jesus was crucified and rose from the dead (verses 23-24)

His death and resurrection were predicted in the Bible (verses 25-35)

Jesus was the long-awaited Messiah (verse 36)

Repent and be baptized (verses 37-38)

Three thousand believed and were baptized (verse 41)

Saul

The Persecutor of Christians

*"Saul, Saul, why are you persecuting Me?" And
[Paul] said, "Who are You, Lord?" Then the Lord
said, "I am Jesus, whom you are persecuting."*
ACTS 9:4-5

☨

Most notable quality: Zeal
Most notable accomplishment: Church planter and writer of
13 New Testament books
Date lived: A.D. 1 to A.D. 67
Name: *Saul,* meaning "asked"
Major text: Acts 9:1-30

Bare Bones Background

In the Roman Empire, each nation and ethnic group is given the opportunity to live under their own laws as long as those laws do not interfere with the best interests of Rome. This means that a young Pharisee by the name of Saul is acting within the guidelines of Roman law as he leads in the persecution of those suspected of violating Jewish religious law. It is also within the authority of the Jewish religious council known as the Sanhedrin to send Saul to Damascus to capture and bring back to Jerusalem those who violate Jewish law. It is while Saul is on this journey to Damascus that he encounters the risen Savior, Jesus Christ.

Quick Sketch

Born about A.D. 1 in Tarsus, a city in Asia Minor, Saul receives his initial training at the local Greek university. Then, as is the custom of devout Jewish families, his parents send Paul to Jerusalem to stay with relatives (Acts 23:16) and complete his training in the orthodoxy traditions of Judaism, under the teaching of Gamaliel, the most respected teacher in the land. This training prepares Saul to become a member of the most zealous religious group in Judah, a Pharisee. His training, abilities, and zeal quickly elevate him, even as a young man of thirtyish, to a position of respect and authority in the Jewish council called the Sanhedrin. Saul then gains permission of the local Roman authorities to begin a ruthless campaign of stamping out the "heretics" who claim Jesus as their Messiah.

The Big Picture

▶ **Saul's zeal as a persecutor**—*Acts 7:1–8:3*

Saul is present when Stephen, the young evangelist, is brought before the Sanhedrin and boldly explains from biblical history that their forefathers had repeatedly resisted rather than responded to God. He argues that the Sanhedrin's approval of the crucifixion of Jesus is yet another of those occasions when they resisted the Holy Spirit (7:51). Stephen's reproach turns the council into an angry mob that drags him outside the city, where they stone him to death. Saul approves of the mob's actions and watches over their garments while they stone Stephen (7:58). Stephen's death begins an intense persecution of the new church—a persecution of which Saul is a leader as he goes from house to house dragging off men and women to prison (8:1-3). Fleeing for their lives, the large Jewish Christian population in Jerusalem is scattered throughout the Roman Empire. Many go to Damascus, the capital of Syria, 160 miles northeast of Jerusalem.

▶ **Saul's conversion**—*Acts 9:1-12*

Saul starts by persecuting Christians in Jerusalem, then asks for permission to go to Damascus to continue his mission of rooting out this heresy as it spreads. As Saul and his party are nearing the end of their journey, Saul is blinded by a flash of brilliant light, and hears Jesus speaking from heaven. He realizes that those whom he has been persecuting are right: Jesus is the Messiah, the Son of God! Blinded as a result of the light, Saul is led the rest of the way to Damascus by his traveling companions.

▶ **Saul's new mission**—*Acts 9:13-30*

The Lord informs Ananias, in a vision, that Saul will now be His spokesman to carry the message of Jesus' resurrection to the Gentiles, to kings, and to the children of Israel throughout the Roman Empire. Ananias prays for Saul, and Saul's sight is restored. Saul is baptized immediately and becomes as bold and zealous in preaching Christ as he had been in persecuting Christ's followers.

▶ **Saul's preparation**—*Galatians 1:17-18*

Saul spends three years in Damascus and the Arabian desert poring over the Old Testament scriptures and being taught by the "revelation of Jesus Christ" (Galatians 1:12). He begins to grasp the significance of Christ's death and resurrection. Paul returns to Damascus, where he "confounded the Jews...proving that this Jesus is the Christ" (verse 22). Saul's aggressive preaching arouses so much hostility in Damascus that the Christians lower him over the wall of the city at night to save his life.

Saul returns to Jerusalem after three years of absence. At first the believers are afraid of him. It is only after Barnabas brings Saul to the church leadership that Saul is finally accepted. Soon Saul's zeal for preaching Christ arouses hostility in Jerusalem, making it necessary to send him away—this time to his home town of Tarsus. Some years later, Barnabas, who befriends Saul, will come to Tarsus to recruit Saul to join in the ministry of a predominantly Gentile church in Antioch.

The Portrait

Scripture reveals that Saul, whose name was also Paul, was an extremely intense man. He never did anything in a halfhearted fashion—especially when it came to serving his Lord. What enabled Paul to maintain such spiritual fervor even in the midst of great persecution and pain? At the heart of his zeal was a love of Christ. Once he met the risen Savior, Christ was real to Paul. Jesus had saved him and given him a mission, and at the core of Paul's efforts was a desire to "know [Christ] and the power of His resurrection, and the fellowship of His sufferings, being conformed to His death" (Philippians 3:10).

Life Lessons from Paul

Christ should be the focus of your passion. Paul was a man of passion when it came to God. Before he met Christ on the Damascus road, Paul was fervent in his persecution of those whom he thought were perverting God's law. Then after meeting Christ, he was just as passionate, but from this point onward his passion was focused on Christ. What about you? Your outward passion reveals what is most important in your heart. Has your love for the Savior cooled over the years? If you have "left your first love" (Revelation 2:4), ask the Lord to help you renew the passion that was once so zealous.

Never lose sight of your calling. In the years that followed his conversion Paul continued to talk about his experience on the road to Damascus. He shared extensively about his conversion experience with a Jewish mob in Jerusalem (Acts 22:6-16) and with King Agrippa (Acts 26:12-19). Each time, Paul affirmed he had not lost sight of his calling (verse 19). To Paul, Jesus was as vivid as when he first met Him. Are you still excited about your conversion? How often do you relate to others the details about how and when you met Jesus? Ask God for a fresh sense of His calling and saving work in your life. Never lose sight of your calling to serve Jesus—be faithful to share your salvation experience with any and all who come across your path.

Jesus is asking you to suffer for Him. Paul was told he would be required to suffer for Jesus. Almost immediately this prediction became a reality for Paul. Jesus tells us as well that in this world, we will have tribulation (John 16:33). Later Paul would write to a young pastor friend, saying, "All who desire to live godly in Christ Jesus will suffer persecution" (2 Timothy 3:12). Are you experiencing some form of persecution for your faith? Don't be surprised. Jesus said it would come. If you are not presently experiencing persecution, be thankful, but also be concerned.

Check the temperature of your heart. Is it on fire for Jesus? The world doesn't bother with "lukewarm" Christians.

Paul's Five Visits to Jerusalem

1. First visit—comes after his conversion and three years in Damascus and the Arabian Desert (Acts 9:26-30).

2. Second visit—Paul and Barnabas bring relief money from the Antioch church. They then return to Antioch and take Mark with them (Acts 11:27-30).

3. Third visit—Paul and Barnabas return with others from the Antiochian church to debate at the Jerusalem council (Acts 15; Galatians 2) the issue of Gentile Christians and the rituals of Judaism. They take Titus, as an example of a Gentile Christian who has never been exposed to Jewish law.

4. Fourth visit—Paul and his team come for a brief visit (Acts 18:22), leaving behind, in Ephesus, his friends Priscilla and Aquila.

5. Fifth visit—at the end of his third missionary journey, Paul and his team travel to Jerusalem with a monetary collection gathered from the churches of Asia Minor (Acts 21). Paul is arrested and spends his remaining years in jail (Acts 21–28).

Paul

The Apostle to the Gentiles

*But rise and stand on your feet; for I have
appeared to you for this purpose, to make
you a minister and a witness both of the
things which you have seen and of the
things which I will yet reveal to you.*
ACTS 26:16

⚛

Most notable quality: Passion for Christ
Most notable accomplishment: Wrote 13 books of the New
Testament
Date lived: A.D. 1 to A.D. 67
Name: *Paul*, meaning "little"
Major texts: Acts 12:25–28:31; Paul's letters

Bare Bones Background

The formation of the church on the Day of Pentecost is mostly a Jewish
affair. The vast majority of early believers in Jerusalem are converted
Jews, and Jesus is the long-awaited Messiah of the Jews. Initially, Gentiles
were of no consideration. It is only after Stephen's death and the outbreak
of persecution that the new church begins to fulfill Christ's commission
to take His message to "the end of the earth" (Acts 1:8)—which means
taking the message to non-Jews, or Gentiles.

Philip is among those who are forced to leave Jerusalem. He
preaches to the Samaritans, and to an Ethiopian man (Acts 8:26-39).

Peter is called by God to preach to a Roman named Cornelius (Acts 10:34-43). Each group of people—the Samaritans, the Romans, and Cornelius and his household—receive the Holy Spirit. The Jews in Jerusalem are utterly amazed that God would extend salvation to the Gentiles as well.

The Jewish leadership also hears about a group of Greeks who have fled from Jerusalem and who were preaching the gospel to Gentiles in Antioch of Syria. Again they are astonished that a great number of Gentiles are coming to Christ and that a church has been formed. They send Barnabas to check out this amazing news. It is now time for the apostle to the Gentiles, Paul, to enter the scene.

Quick Sketch

Saul, the reformed Christian killer, is an aggressive preacher who comes to Jerusalem from Damascus, where he had seen a vision of Jesus. His confrontational style stirs up much hostility and great turmoil in the city. In an attempt to calm things down the Jewish Christians put Saul onto a ship bound for his hometown of Tarsus. This begins a second period of silence in the life of Saul, who will later take on his Greek name, Paul (the first period of silence was Saul's time in the Arabian desert).

It is at this point that we begin to understand that God does not waste any of Paul's unique qualities as He is about to send this specially equipped man as a missionary to the Gentiles. Here are some of Paul's credentials:

Paul is a Roman citizen—He has unrestricted freedom to travel throughout the Roman Empire. As a Roman citizen, he is protected from Jewish prosecution for religious matters. He cannot be punished without a trial. Roman citizenship would also allow him to mingle with all levels of society in every place to which he travels.

Paul is educated in Greek—He is able to write and speak the universal trade language of the empire. His education also gives him the ability to arrange his theological arguments in the logical Greek fashion of thinking.

Paul is educated in Jewish law—Paul has been trained by one of the most respected teachers in Judaism, Gamaliel. He is an expert in the Old Testament scriptures.

Paul is taught by the Holy Spirit—After his conversion, Paul spends time in the Arabian Desert, where he receives the revelation needed to understand and communicate God's plan of salvation through the Lord Jesus Christ. Paul's understanding of the "deep things of God" will enable him to put, in written form, teachings that are the basis of Christian theology.

Paul is bivocational—He is a trained tentmaker. This skill proves valuable during those times when Paul needs financial support for himself and his team. He will never be accused of using the gospel for his own profit.

Paul is experienced—By the time God sends Paul out to preach to the Gentiles, he has been preaching and serving for about ten years in Damacus, Jerusalem, Tarsus, and Antioch. Paul will carry on as the apostle to the Gentiles for more than 20 years before he is martyred in Rome by Nero.

The Big Picture

▶ **Paul the missionary**—*Acts 13–28*

Paul's strategy:

—travel to major population centers along established travel routes

—preach of the Messiah to Jews first in their synagogues along with God-fearing Gentiles

—move on to Gentile audiences if the Jews resist

—instruct a core group of believers in the faith

—leave behind a church and repeat the process

—revisit the churches or write letters of instruction to them

▶ **Paul the theologian**—*his 13 epistles*

Paul is a profound theologian, as witnessed by his epistle to the Romans. It has been referred to as the greatest theological treatise of all times—the righteousness of God is its theme. Yet Romans and Paul's other 12 epistles (letters) are as much practical as they are theological. He writes letters to real people who are struggling with real problems. His challenge is to explain the great truths of God in such a way as to show their practical implications for daily living. His letters teach spiritual truths that transform lives—truths about knowing and walking with God and how this knowledge helps his readers put their relationships in fresh and transforming perspective.

The Portrait

Next to our Lord Jesus, Paul was the most significant figure of the Christian era. He possessed great intellectual gifts and an unusually strong will. In his early years as a Christian he exhibited some rough edges. Later on, as you read his letters, you see a softer, more gentle person. Paul had grown in his love for his Savior and for God's people. He was willing to pay any price to serve God and others—even when that price was personal suffering and pain. He was still as bold as ever in taking stands for what was right. He was still a demanding leader, and he was still uncompromising in his convictions. Yet even in his confrontations, Paul exhibited a maturing love and compassion for those who were without Christ. Here are some more qualities Paul possessed:

He invested in the lives of others.

He was a team player.

He was an encourager.

He was a motivator.

He brought out the best in people.

He modeled what he preached.

He did not ask of others what he wasn't willing to do himself.

History has shown that Paul was the primary architect of Christian theology, having been tutored by God's Spirit in the significance of Christ's death and the nature of the new life to be lived "in Christ." He was also the chief model for biblical missionary strategy.

Life Lessons from Paul

God has uniquely prepared you for His service. Paul had an incredible impact on the world of his day. His unique life, his great intellect, his education, and his training were valuable assets in God's hands. Nothing was left behind at his salvation but his sin. God used Paul's unique gifts and skills for His glory, but He also had a ready servant in Paul. Nothing was off limits to God in Paul's life. You too have a unique set of gifts and abilities that make you of great value for God's service. Are you willing to let God take your life—with all its qualities—and use it for His service? Or are there areas of your life that you are holding back for yourself? You will never know all that He can do through you until you allow Him to have every part of you.

Praise should be at the heart of your relationships. Paul understood the value of well-timed words of encouragement. In every one of his letters, he took time to praise the efforts of others—such as his praise of Tychicus in Ephesians 6:21: "Tychicus, a beloved brother and faithful minister in the Lord...." To be affirmed publicly is a great motivator. Do you notice the efforts of others? How quick are you to give praise to them for those efforts? Do you go out of your way to praise the accomplishments of fellow workers? Make it a goal today to affirm everyone you come in contact with. Watch the difference a few words of praise will make!

Adversity is an opportunity for you to trust God. Paul prayed three times for God to remove what he called his "thorn in the flesh" (2 Corinthians 12:7). Finally, Paul understood what God was doing: The problem kept him humble, forced him to depend on God, and shaped his character. Are you suffering from your own particular "thorn," whether it's a debilitating illness, a financial reversal, or a malicious attack on your character? Remember to ask *what* rather than *why.* God understands your pain and has reasons for your suffering. Turn your thorn into trust. Use your adversity as an opportunity to trust God and understand *what* He wants to teach you as you go through your situation. As in Paul's life, God's grace is sufficient even for your problem!

Paul's Prison Experiences

Paul spent many days, weeks, months, and years in prison for his faith.

- The Philippian jail—overnight (Acts 16:22-40)
- Unrecorded frequent imprisonments (2 Corinthians 11:23)
- The provincial jail at Caesarea—two years (A.D. 57–59) (Traveling to Rome in chains to stand before Caesar—fall A.D. 59–Spring A.D. 60) (Acts 27–28)
- The first Roman imprisonment—two years (A.D. 60–62) (Awaiting trial before Caesar under "house arrest"—Paul was then freed and traveled to various churches) (A.D. 62–65)
- The second Roman imprisonment (A.D. 67) (Much more severe treatment, which ended in martyrdom.)

Timothy

A Trainer of the Next Generation

The things that you have heard from me
among many witnesses, commit these to faithful
men who will be able to teach others also.
2 TIMOTHY 2:2

☙

Most notable quality: A faithful man
Most notable accomplishment: Paul's representative to the
churches
Date lived: Mid-first century
Name: *Timothy,* meaning "honored by God"
Major texts: Acts 16:1-3; 17:14-15; 1 Corinthians 4:17; 1 and 2
Timothy

Bare Bones Background

While Paul and Barnabas, along with others, are about the business
of teaching and ministering to the Christians at Antioch of Syria, the Holy
Spirit speaks to the leadership. Paul and Barnabas are to be set apart for
special missionary service. The congregation, with its leadership, pray,
fast, and send two of their most capable and gifted leaders from Antioch
on the first of three missionary journeys. Ultimately they will arrive at
the far end of their trip in the area called Galatia (modern Turkey) and
the towns of Derby and Lystra.

Upon their arrival, Paul and his team begin their usual practice of
preaching about Jesus. There is no mention of a Jewish meeting place,

or a synagogue, so Paul preaches to the crowds in the marketplace. It is at one of these marketplace meetings that a young boy named Timothy, his mother, Eunice, and grandmother, Lois, may have become Christians. After a time of instruction, Paul and Barnabas leave behind a fledgling church.

Quick Sketch

Several years later Paul, along with his new traveling companion, Silas, retrace their steps from the first missionary trip. Once again they come to Timothy's hometown of Derbe. Timothy is known by Paul from his first journey. Hearing that Timothy is now older (possibly in his mid-twenties) and well spoken of by the Christians in the area, Paul asks Timothy to join the team as his apprentice. Timothy is ideally suited for missionary service because he has a Greek father and a Jewish mother. This combination will give him access to both Gentile and Jewish cultures.

As the years progress Timothy shows himself to be a faithful and loyal follower of Paul. On frequent occasions Timothy is asked by Paul to carry communications between congregations where Paul has ministered. Toward the end of his life, Paul sends Timothy to Ephesus, a church that Paul planted, as his official representative to assist in the appointing and training of leader. It is while Timothy is at Ephesus that he receives two letters of encouragement and instruction from Paul, who is now a prisoner in Rome. These two letters, 1 and 2 Timothy, provide a lasting record of Paul's love and concern for Timothy and his philosophy of ministry for a local church.

The Big Picture

▶ **Timothy's early life**—*2 Timothy 1:5; 3:15*

Paul, in his second letter to Timothy, gives us a picture of Timothy's early life as he reminds Timothy of his strong faith, which was first evidenced in his mother, Eunice, and his grandmother, Lois. These two women had been faithful to instruct Timothy in the Old Testament Scriptures since he was a young lad at home. It was these "Holy Scriptures" (3:15) that had prepared him for faith in Jesus Christ.

▶ Timothy as Paul's companion

Timothy joins Paul's missionary team and spends the next 15-plus years helping Paul. Here is how these years are filled:

- Timothy travels with Paul to Philippi, where he begins to display his devotion to Paul and his evangelistic zeal (Philippians 2:22). He is left behind to watch over the newly formed church while Paul moves on to Thessalonica (Acts 17:1).

- Paul and Silas preach in Thessalonica long enough to plant a church. When trouble erupts, Paul and Silas travel to Berea. Again when trouble ignites, Paul moves on to Athens, while Silas remains to wait for Timothy.

- Timothy arrives from Philippi and remains with Silas in Thessalonica as they teach and preach to the newly formed church (Acts 17:14).

- Timothy and Silas join Paul in Athens, where Paul sends Timothy back to Thessalonica to "establish [them] and encourage [them] concerning [their] faith" (1 Thessalonians 3:2).

- He travels back to meet up with Paul in Corinth, which is south of Athens (Acts 18:5). He is with Paul as he writes two letters to the Thessalonian church (1 and 2 Thessalonians 1:1).

- Timothy is not mentioned again for about five years, until he is sent from Ephesus to Greece to prepare for Paul's coming (Acts 19:22). He travels with Paul to Corinth and is with him as the apostle writes to the believers in Rome (16:21).

- Timothy is not mentioned again until he arrives in Rome to be with Paul during his imprisonment and the writing of what are called his "prison epistles."

- Timothy travels with Paul after his release and is reluctantly left in Ephesus (2 Timothy 1:4) to deal with problems related to false doctrine, disorder in worship, the need for mature leaders, and worldliness. While in Greece, Paul writes Timothy the first of two letters to address these issues. A second letter comes shortly afterward, but this time from a cell in Rome, where Paul will soon be martyred. Paul asks Timothy to join him as soon as possible.

The Portrait

Long before Paul first arrived in Derbe, Timothy had been well schooled in the Old Testament scriptures by his mother and grandmother. God opened up those scriptures in Timothy's heart and mind as Paul preached about Jesus the Messiah. Timothy continued to grow and mature in Paul's absence. He was biblically and culturally qualified to join Paul's team, and Paul saw great potential in him. Paul demonstrated his confidence in Timothy by entrusting him with important responsibilities. Timothy seems to have been reserved and oftentimes timid. His youthfulness didn't help, as the churches often looked down upon his age as he brought them instructions from Paul. While Paul is awaiting execution, he asks Timothy to come to him in Rome. It is uncertain whether Timothy was able to reach Paul before his death.

Timothy himself suffered at least one imprisonment after the death of Paul—we know this because the writer of Hebrews recorded his release (Hebrews 13:23). There is no further biblical record of Timothy's ministry or death, but tradition states that he continued his ministry in Ephesus and suffered martyrdom during the reign of Domitian (A.D. 81–96), emperor of Rome.

Life Lessons from Timothy

Realize the importance of training the next generation of leaders. Paul was a trainer of men. He mentored and sent out many young men. He knew that his one life would soon be over, so he did what he could to raise up men like Timothy, who would carry on the faith. Are you following in Paul's footsteps? Who are those you are training to be the next generation of "on fire" Christians? Start with your children, then look to other young people in your church. Young women need training in godly behavior. Young men need to learn how to lead in their future homes. How else will the next generation learn if you don't teach them?

Give young people opportunities to develop their spiritual gifts. Timothy, from the very start of his missionary tour with Paul, was given chances to put his faith into practice. He rose to the occasions and soon caught a vision of what God was able to do in and through him. He went on to play a vital role in the growth and development of the early church. Young people need close guidance, but they also need the freedom and opportunities to put their faith to work and to discover their spiritual gifts. Just as you teach your children how to discover their natural talents and abilities, teach your children and other young people how to serve God and discover their spiritual gifts.

Remember the role of parents in spiritual development. It is obvious how important Lois and Eunice were in the spiritual development of young Timothy. As a parent, you have no idea the extent of your influence when it comes to spiritual matters. Timothy's mother and grandmother had a "genuine faith," a true undistorted faith—not a hypocritical faith, not a Sunday faith. Theirs was the real deal and was lived out in front of Timothy. Make sure your faith is a genuine faith that is lived out before your children. This is the greatest help you can give to your children or other young people as they struggle toward spiritual growth and maturity.

Other Men Who Traveled with Paul

Titus—a Greek convert who was entrusted with missions to Corinth and Crete (2 Corinthians 2:13; 7:6-15; 8:6,16-24; book of Titus)

Tychicus—an Asian Christian who served as Paul's messenger to many of the churches

Epaphras—came to Christ at Ephesus and then founded the Colossian church. He was so concerned with heresies that were creeping into his church that he made the long journey to Rome to ask for Paul's help with certain doctrinal issues.

Epaphroditus—a member of the Philippian church who brought to Paul some gifts from the church and became deathly ill while with Paul

Aquila and Priscilla
A Dynamic Duo

Greet Priscilla and Aquila, my fellow workers
in Christ Jesus, who risked their own necks
for my life, to whom not only I give thanks,
but also all the churches of the Gentiles. Like-
wise greet the church that is in their house.
ROMANS 16:3-5

☩

Most notable quality: Willing servants
Most notable accomplishment: Risked their lives for Paul
Date lived: Middle of the first century
Name: *Aquila*, meaning "eagle," and *Priscilla*, meaning "worthy" or "venerable"
Major text: Acts 18

Bare Bones Background

After Julius Caesar, Claudius was the Emperor of Rome. The Jews were generally treated with indifference during his reign, except for a time in A.D. 49, when he expelled all Jews from Rome (Acts 18:2). It is at this time that a couple by the names of Aquila and Priscilla leave Rome and make their way to Corinth, a great commercial city, where they begin doing business as tentmakers. Paul, a fellow tentmaker, becomes friends with this couple, who probably had become Christians in Rome and had been members of the church in that city.

Quick Sketch

Aquila and Priscilla are a remarkable husband-and-wife team. In Scripture, they are always mentioned together. Together, they make tents. And together, they befriend Paul, who is also a tentmaker, and accompany him on his missionary journeys. Their home is always open to others, and they hold church services in their home in every place they live. They are learners as they sit under the teaching of Paul. And together, they are teachers, taking what they have learned and passing it on to others. Even when it comes to danger and courage, they are mentioned together by Paul as they "risked their own necks" for him. Paul is so deeply grateful for their friendship and partnership in the gospel that he openly expresses his appreciation for their service in his letter to the church in Rome, where they are living at that time (Romans 16:3-5).

The Big Picture

A brief overview of this amazing couple reveals two people who were intertwined in a mutual life of service.

They are available—Each time Priscilla and Aquila are mentioned in the Bible, they are either in or on their way to a different city and involving themselves in various acts of service:

Acts 18:1-3—They open their home to Paul and share their place of trade with him as fellow tentmakers.

Acts 18:18-19—They are Paul's traveling companions as he moves from Corinth to Ephesus.

Acts 18:24-28—They help complete the training of Apollos, a man who knew only of the teachings of John the Baptist. He went on to become a great preacher for Christ.

Romans 16:3-5—They have a church meeting in their home in Rome.

1 Corinthians 16:19—They have a church meeting in their home in Ephesus.

They are hospitable—They housed Paul for over a year when he came to Corinth. They also opened their home for the new church in Ephesus, and again later in Rome.

They are knowledgeable—Having lived and worked with the great apostle Paul for months, Aquila and Priscilla are well versed in Scripture. This is demonstrated by how they "took [Apollos] aside and explained to him the way of God more accurately" (Acts 18:26).

They are fearless—Being a Christian in the early days of the church is very dangerous. There is much persecution of believers by the Roman government and local pagan religious groups. Paul is an expert at receiving persecution, having been beaten, stoned, imprisoned, and generally mistreated everywhere he goes. This amazing couple experience much of the same treatment, as they "risked their own necks" for Paul.

The Portrait

Together Priscilla and Aquila worked as tentmakers. They knew and shared the teachings of Christ, opened their home to others, and encountered life-threatening persecution. What a couple! They were constantly on the move from place to place. But their eyes and ears, not to mention their hearts, were open to those in need. They were ready, willing, and able—at least with what little they had—to serve the Lord anywhere, in any way, at any time, and at any cost. They were an incredible example of what it means to serve the Lord as a couple.

Life Lessons from Aquila and Priscilla

Effective service as a couple requires that each is growing spiritually—Priscilla and Aquila were both learning and growing spiritually under the ministry of Paul. When it came time to give further information on the Christian faith, both were prepared to give Apollos more accurate information. Whether you are a husband or a wife, be growing in the Lord yourself, and encourage your spouse to be growing, too. God gave you to each other to be a greater force together than either of you by yourself. To work well as a team, you must both be growing as individuals.

Effective service starts with the little things—Priscilla and Aquila started by opening their home to Paul. They didn't need any training on how to show hospitality. It was Paul's teaching that prepared them to instruct Apollos with more accurate information. And that's true for you as well. It's a little thing to sweep the floors at church, pick up after the Sunday service, help with repairs around the church, or to provide meals for the sick. As you grow in your faith and get a better understanding of your spiritual gifts and are faithful in the little things, you will also grow in your capability for service in bigger things.

Effective service is possible when you make yourself available— Priscilla and Aquila had a full life of service because they were available. It appears that they had no children, so the opportunities for ministry were greatly increased. There are times and seasons when you will find yourself limited by family and work obligations, but this should be no excuse for failing to use your spiritual gifts in some capacity. Make your best effort to make yourself available to God, and watch Him multiply the effects of your service.

A Biblical Understanding of Service

Service is expected—you were created for good works (Ephesians 2:10).

Service must be undivided—you cannot serve two masters (Luke 16:13).

Service is to be sacrificial—service that counts is service that costs (Romans 12:1).

Service is to benefit others—God has given you spiritual gifts to serve His body, the church (1 Corinthians 12:7).

Titus

Paul's Mirror Image

Thanks be to God who puts the same earnest care for you into the heart of Titus...If anyone inquires about Titus, he is my partner and fellow worker concerning you...
2 CORINTHIANS 8:16,23

&

Most notable quality: Dependability
Most notable accomplishment: Provided leadership for the churches on the island of Crete
Date lived: Middle to late first century
Name: *Titus*, a common Greek name
Major text: Titus 1–3

Bare Bones Background

Paul is educated, an excellent teacher, highly motivated, and filled with the Holy Spirit. His gifts and abilities make him a dynamic force in the expansion of the gospel and the planting of churches during the formative years of Christianity. But Paul knows that the church must be built on Christ and not personalities. He also knows that the churches need well-trained spiritual leadership if they are to prosper. He knows that he is just one man and that soon he will be gone. Others must be trained up to assume the role of building, encouraging, teaching, and disciplining. To accomplish this, he trains young pastors to assume leadership in the churches after he is gone. Titus is one of the young men being trained by Paul to preach God's Word (2 Timothy 3:16-17) and to train others (2 Timothy 2:2) to carry on the ministry after he is gone.

Quick Sketch

Titus is a Greek believer taught and trained by Paul. When the controversy over the elements involving the salvation of Gentiles erupted, Titus went with Paul to Jerusalem to demonstrate that it is not necessary for a Gentile to keep the Jewish law in order to be saved. Like Timothy, Titus is a trusted traveling companion and friend to Paul. As he matures in the faith, Titus is given the assignment to settle the difficult issues that have erupted in the church in Corinth. Finally, as Paul's life draws to a close, Titus is left in Crete to oversee all the churches on the island and to appoint and train leaders. Paul is sending at least one replacement, Artemas or Tychicus, so that Titus can meet Paul at Nicopolis, a city in southern Greece where Paul plans to spend the winter. Tradition states that Titus later returned to Crete and became the permanent spiritual leader on Crete and died there at an advanced age.

The Big Picture

▶ Titus is introduced—*Galatians 2:1,3*

Titus is a Gentile convert from Antioch who becomes an associate of the apostle Paul. He joins Paul and Barnabas when they travel to Jerusalem and serves as "Exhibit A" concerning Gentile salvation. (Some Jews believed that Gentile converts needed to conform to Jewish law, which included submitting to circumcision.) Titus is Paul's proof that keeping the law should not be required of Gentiles.

▶ Titus is a troubleshooter—*2 Corinthians*

Corinth was Paul's most difficult ministry. There always seemed to be problems in the church there. After Paul's first visit of 18 months, the apostle sends Timothy with 1 Corinthians to address issues of concern. Things seem to have gone from bad to worse, as Paul found it necessary to send Titus from Ephesus to Corinth with the letter 2 Corinthians:

- Paul sends Titus to Corinth with a now-lost letter written "with many tears" (2:4), hoping for repentance from those in sin (7:5-16).

- Paul leaves Ephesus and travels to Troas hoping to meet Titus with news from Corinth. Even though there is a great door of opportunity for ministry, Paul is anxious for news, so he leaves and backtracks to Macedonia looking for Titus (2:12-13).

- Titus and Paul meet in Macedonia. To Paul's relief and joy, Titus brings news that the majority had repented of their rebellion against Paul (7:5-12).

- Paul wants to deal with any smoldering rebellion that is still left, so he writes 2 Corinthians and has it delivered by Titus, along with an unnamed traveling companion—possibly Luke.

- Titus takes 2 Corinthians to Corinth, but not out of obligation. On his own initiative and out of concern, Titus volunteers to return to Corinth to assist Paul in his appeal to the Corinthians to resume their collection for the poor at Jerusalem (8–9).

▶ **Titus is a leader**—*Titus 1–3*

Paul trusted Titus, more than any of his other young men, to be able to solve problems and to make progress under difficult circumstances. This is why Paul leaves Titus on the island of Crete—to complete the task of strengthening the newly planted churches. The island is plagued with immorality and the inhabitants are liars and lazy gluttons. So, the task is a difficult one. Titus's first task is to appoint leaders. Paul gives Titus a list of the qualities needed in leaders, which presupposes that Titus met these qualifications himself. Paul is confident in Titus's leadership ability and his understanding of theological issues, so his letter is more of a reminder of the importance of Christian conduct, especially when it comes to doing good works. Church order and right living are the best evangelistic tools we can possess for a watching world.

The Portrait

Titus made a profound impact on the early church. He was a faithful and skilled man of God whom the apostle Paul entrusted great responsibility. He was given assignments that even Paul's favored associate, Timothy, could not handle. Titus was such a strong and dedicated team member that Paul could rely on him for critical tasks—such as when Timothy could not get the Corinthians to accept Paul. Titus was sent and achieved the desired results. And when Paul needed to leave the island of Crete, Titus was asked to stay behind to finish what Paul had started with the newly planted churches. Titus, in other words, was a man whom Paul could rely on to complete even the most difficult of tasks. Why? Because Titus walked in the same spirit and in the same steps as his teacher (2 Corinthians 12:18).

Life Lessons from Titus

Reliability is essential for service—Titus had a profound impact on the early church. Because of his influence, the churches under his care took root and grew. Titus was such a strong and dedicated servant that Paul could rely on him for many critical tasks. How reliable are you? Can others in the church count on you to do what you say you will do, or be where you say you will be? Faithfulness and reliability are hallmarks of spiritual maturity. You too can have a great influence in your church and your community by just being reliable—a person whom people can depend on.

Problems are a fact of life—The apostle Paul lived a very difficult life. He was always dealing with problems and problem people. But on many occasions he would send others, especially Titus, to bring resolution to a situation. Follow Titus's example the next time you are facing a problem:

- *Accept the reality of your problem*—Titus went to Corinth knowing full well the difficult situation he would face regarding sin. Don't ignore a problem, hoping it will go away. Face your problem frankly.

- *Ascertain the extent of your problem*—Titus was left in Crete to complete a difficult mission. Paul wrote the epistle of Titus to help give Titus the "big picture" of the island and its people and history. Paul's understanding would help Titus to better know how to deal with the churches in Crete. In the same way, make sure you get all the facts. Determine your options. Many problems have more than one solution. Determine all the possibilities.

- *Ask advice from others*—Having seen the problems firsthand, Paul did not hesitate to give advice to Titus. This would enable Titus to make informed decisions. Once you have a good understanding of a problem and have determined your options, it's time to make a decision. Start by asking God for wisdom from His Word. Then ask a wise person in your church for his or her advice. Often an outsider can see an issue more clearly. Only a fool shuns the counsel of others, especially from God! Do you desire wisdom in dealing with the problem before you? Seek to gain that wisdom from others. Then work to solve your problem successfully.

The Profile of a Disciple

Titus walked in Paul's steps—he was a true disciple.

Titus honored Paul like a son to a father—he was a trusted son.

Titus was a willing student—he was a teachable servant.

Titus was focused in his assignment—he was a task-oriented specialist.

Titus was prepared for the most difficult situations—he was a trained soldier in God's army.

Philemon
A Man with a Decision to Make

Having confidence in your
obedience, I write to you, knowing that
you will do even more than I say.
PHILEMON 21

&

Most notable quality: An obedient spirit
Most notable accomplishment: The hearts of the saints
were refreshed by him
Date lived: Middle to late first century
Name: *Philemon*, meaning "friendship"
Major text: Book of Philemon

Bare Bones Background

Slavery is widespread in the Roman Empire. Some have estimated
that slaves constituted at least one-third of the empire's population. In
Paul's day, slaves could be doctors, musicians, teachers, artists, and
many other vocations. Some slaves enjoyed favorable situations and had
a better life than many working-class freemen. But also there were many
slaves who were cruelly treated.

The New Testament nowhere directly attacks slavery. For it to do so
would have resulted in an insurrection, and the gospel message would
have been hopelessly confused with social reform. Christianity's influence on society began to undermine the evils of slavery by changing the
hearts of both slaves and their masters. Spiritual change should produce

social change. Paul's letter to a slave owner named Philemon concerning Philemon's runaway slave, Onesimus, brings this transforming process to light.

Quick Sketch

Philemon is a wealthy member of the church in Colosse, a city about 100 miles east of Ephesus. Philemon probably had become a Christian under Paul's three-year ministry in Ephesus during his third missionary journey. Philemon is affluent enough to own at least one slave, a man named Onesimus. Paul addresses a letter to Philemon and also writes to Apphia and Archippus, his wife and son, as well as the church that meets in their home. Paul wants this personal letter read in the church. This public reading would hold Philemon accountable and also instruct the church on the matter of forgiveness.

The Big Picture

▶ Onesimus's crime

Onesimus is not a believer when he steals some money (verse 18) from Philemon and flees to Rome, hoping to lose himself in the large slave population of the city. By the providence of God, Onesimus meets Paul in Rome and becomes a Christian. Paul quickly grows fond of Onesimus (verses 12,16) and desires to keep him in Rome because of his usefulness to Paul while he is in prison (verse 11).

▶ Paul's problem

Onesimus has broken Roman law by stealing from his master and running away. Paul knows that he must return Onesimus to his master. Both he and Onesimus know that the law allows an owner the right to kill a runaway slave. Paul sends Philemon a letter asking Philemon to forgive Onesimus and welcome him back to serve as a brother in Christ (verses 15-17). It is too dangerous for Onesimus to make the trip alone because of slave-catchers, so Paul sends him back with Tychicus, who is returning to Colosse with the letter to the Colossians (Colossians 4:7-9). And as a final note, Paul expresses hope that he will soon be released from prison and asks Philemon to prepare a guest room in anticipation of his visit.

▶ Philemon's opportunity to forgive

Paul's appeal to Philemon to forgive Onesimus is based on these relationships:

- Philemon's relationship to Paul—Paul is an old and suffering friend who led Philemon to saving faith, a debt Philemon could never repay.

- Philemon's relationship with Jesus—Philemon is full of love and faith for Jesus, who has forgiven him.

- Philemon's relationship to his fellow believers—Philemon has opened his heart and home to others...so why not Onesimus?

- Onesimus's relationship with Jesus—Onesimus is now a fellow believer in Jesus.

- Onesimus's relationship to Philemon—Onesimus is no longer useless, but useful.

- Paul's relationship to Philemon—Paul offers to pay whatever money is necessary for Onesimus to be reconciled to Philemon.

The Portrait

All that we know of Philemon's character is described in this short letter. He was depicted as one with great nobility. He was commended for his faith and love, his generosity and hospitality, his obedience and forgiving spirit. Philemon had been transformed on the vertical level by his relationship with God, which should have resulted in a transformation on the horizontal level in his relationships with others—particularly Onesimus. We have no indication how Philemon received this letter, but given Paul's tactful persuasion and Philemon's transformed Christian character, we can only venture a guess that Onesimus was reconciled to Philemon, and that a new era of slave and master relationships began...at least in this one church.

Life Lessons from Philemon

Forgiveness is most Christlike when given to the undeserving—Philemon had the law on his side. Onesimus had broken the law and deserved to be punished. Yet Paul asked Philemon to forgive out of love for Christ and his friendship with Paul. In the same way that you have been forgiven in Christ, so you too should freely forgive others whether they deserve it or not. Do you need to forgive someone who has wronged you? Or do you need to ask for forgiveness from others? Forgiving others is an indicator that you too have been forgiven in Christ.

Coming to Christ does not relieve you of your past sinful actions—Onesimus had a past. Yes, he was now a believer and forgiven of his past sins, but he still was obligated to answer for his actions. He showed his transformed life by willingly returning and submitting himself to his master's judgment. Is there something in your past that you need to make right? Ask God to give you the courage and strength to do whatever is necessary to repair any broken relationships or undo a wrong you have committed.

Mediating on behalf of others is an important function of your Christian life—Paul was a friend of both Philemon and Onesimus. There was an obvious issue between these two believers. Paul could have used his authority as an apostle to dictate a reconciliation, yet he chose to appeal to Philemon's transformed life and let the decision be Philemon's. Having been reconciled to God yourself, you now have been given a "ministry of reconciliation" (2 Corinthians 5:18). When those occasions arise, follow Paul's example and appeal to the Christian character in others, and allow the Holy Spirit to work in their hearts to do what is right. You may have the power or authority to make others do what is right, but unless they are personally convinced of a resolution, any change will only be superficial.

Divine Labor Relations
Ephesians 6:5-9

Respect and obey your boss.
Serve your boss as you would serve Christ.

Work hard even when the boss is not looking.

See your job as God's will.

Work with joy as if you are working for Christ.

God will reward your hard work.

James

A Servant of Christ

When James, Cephas, and John, who seemed
to be pillars, perceived the grace that had
been given to me, they gave me and
Barnabas the right hand of fellowship.
GALATIANS 2:9

☥

Most notable quality: Humility
Most notable accomplishment: Wrote a New Testament
book bearing his name
Date lived: 3 B.C. to A.D. 62
Name: *James*, meaning "supplanter"
Major texts: Acts 12:17; 15:13,21; Galatians 1:19; 2:9,12

Bare Bones Background

The book of Acts opens with a great change taking place in the small band of believers in Jesus. In the opening few chapters, Jesus sends His promised Spirit upon them, who then empowers the disciples with boldness and courage. Within a few short weeks, thousands more come to believe in Jesus as Messiah through the preaching of the apostles and the other disciples who witnessed the coming of the Holy Spirit.

One of those present is James, the half-brother of Jesus, who only a few short weeks before, was a skeptic and an unbeliever. But James's life is radically changed with a postresurrection visit from Jesus. James now becomes an outspoken follower of Jesus as Messiah. He will devote the rest of his life in service to Jesus, calling himself not the half-brother of Jesus, but "a bondservant of God and of the Lord Jesus Christ" (James 1:1).

Quick Sketch

James is the eldest son of Joseph and Mary. He is the half-brother of Jesus, who was born of Mary. He has three other brothers—Joses, Simon, and Judas (Jude)—and at least two sisters, whose names are never mentioned. Throughout his early life and until the resurrection of Jesus, James is not a believer in Jesus as Messiah. When Jesus appears to James and others after His resurrection (1 Corinthians 15:5,7), James becomes a believer. As the then-eldest brother, James may have played an important role in the conversion of his other brothers, because he and his brothers are with the apostles and others in the upper room after the ascension of Jesus.

James quickly becomes a leader in the church of Jerusalem. By the time Paul returns after his conversion and three years in Damascus, James has received the title of apostle (Galatians 1:19), and is one of only two leaders Paul mentions meeting with on his brief visit to Jerusalem (the other being Peter). After several periods of persecution, during which many Jewish converts are scattered, James writes a letter to encourage these converts. Several years later he presides over the Jerusalem council (Acts 15). Then years later he, along with the elders, receives Paul upon his return from his third missionary tour (Acts 21:18). Tradition has it that James was martyred in A.D. 62 just after the death of the Roman governor Festus, who is mentioned in Acts 24:27–26:32.

The Big Picture

▶ **James the skeptic**—*John 7:1-5*

James and his brothers spend 30 years growing up around Jesus. Daily they are eyewitnesses of His goodness. Their problem is not with Him as a person, but with His claims to be the Messiah, the Savior of Israel. They are not present at the wedding in Cana with their mother when Jesus changes the water into wine. Nor are they present during those months when all Israel seems to respond to His teaching. All they see are the crowds and His claims. Finally they come and try to take Him away from the crowds, thinking He is out of His mind with delusions of grandeur (Mark 3:20-21). Later they encourage Jesus to go to Jerusalem and prove His claims with a display of His miracles. To them, Jerusalem's acceptance of Him would be a deciding factor for their own belief.

▸ James the believer—*Acts 1:14*

The Gospels show James and his brothers as skeptics and scoffers. What changes them? The apostle Paul says James receives a special visitation from the risen Christ (1 Corinthians 15:7) before He returned to heaven. Like Paul, James responds with great vigor. The next mention of James shows him as a believer along with his brothers and their mother, Mary, in the upper room, praying and waiting for the coming of Christ's Spirit to empower them for service.

▸ James the leader—*Acts 12; 15; 21*

Over the next few years James gains acceptance as a man of wisdom and piety. At the time of the death of the apostle James, brother of John, in Acts 12:2, James is already a recognized leader in the church. Peter is put in prison and scheduled for execution just after James's death. In dramatic fashion, Peter is freed from prison by an angel. Before he goes into hiding, Peter acknowledges James's prominence by specifically asking that James, along with others, be notified of his escape.

When a controversy arises in the church and a council is called, James presides as moderator. He gives the third and final speech at the council, supporting the apostles Peter and Paul, who urge that Gentile converts not be forced to keep Jewish laws. The council accepts James's wisdom and agrees not to put a burden of Jewish legalism on Gentile believers (Acts 15:6-21).

Paul continues to recognize James's leadership role when he returns from his third missionary journey and states that he went to "James, and all the elders" (Acts 21:18) with a report of his tour.

▸ James the author—*the book of James*

After Stephen is martyred (Acts 8:1-3, around A.D. 31–34), a major period of persecution breaks out in Jerusalem. Saul, a young Pharisee who would later become the apostle Paul, plays a major role as he goes from house to house, dragging believers off to prison. A large number of Christian Jews are scattered throughout the Roman world. Then another period of persecution erupts when Herod Agrippa (Acts 12, around A.D. 44) has the apostle James killed. Again, believers are scattered. Because the majority of those scattered do not yet have the support of a local church, James writes to them as a concerned leader to encourage them to maintain, during these difficult times, a lifestyle representative of the Christian faith. James's letter is written around A.D. 45 to 49, and is considered to be the earliest of all the New Testament epistles.

The Portrait

Eusebius, the great Christian leader of the second century, described James as a man of distinguished moral excellence. He was given the additional name of "the Just" because of his virtuous character. Tradition describes James as possessing great piety and receiving the nickname of "camel knees" because of the calluses that developed on his knees from spending so much time in prayer.

James's life is somewhat shrouded in mystery, but his letter gives us a brief glimpse into his character. In order to bolster his credibility as an author and leader, James could have described himself as Jesus' brother. Only three other men on the face of the earth could make this claim. Or, he could have boasted that he was one of the chief leaders in a church with thousands of members. Instead, James humbly calls himself a bondslave of God and of Jesus Christ. Even though he was one of the main leaders in Jerusalem, his letter shows the mark of a humble servant of the Lord—a servant who desires his readers to follow in his path of humility and be the proper kind of representative for their Lord.

Life Lessons from James

Salvation is possible for anyone. James was an unbelieving skeptic. He spent years around Jesus and still wasn't convinced. It was only after a visit from the resurrected Jesus that he believed. How many people like James do you have in your life—in your family, at work, or in your neighborhood? No one is beyond salvation. Follow James's advice, and show by your good works that your faith is real. Then pray that the Spirit of Jesus will convict your unbelieving family, friends, and workmates.

Humility is the mark of a true spiritual leader. Jesus said, "Whoever desires to become great among you, let him be your servant" (Matthew 20:26). James didn't demand to be a leader because he was the Lord's half-brother. James's life reminds you that leadership in the church is earned. Your commitment to Jesus as His servant is what gives your life and ministry credibility and respect.

True Christian faith is active. James exhorted his readers, which includes you today, to live out their faith with their actions. Your claim to be a Christian is not valid unless your life produces works of obedient service that validate your words. If you have doubts about the validity of your faith, look at the book of James and the series of tests by which you can measure the genuineness of your faith.

Three Other New Testament Men Named James

James—son of Zebedee,
brother of John,
one of the 12 disciples,
one of the three closest to Jesus,
martyred by Herod A.D. 42

James—son of Alphaeus,
also one of the 12 disciples,
called "the less" possibly because he was younger
than James, the son of Zebedee

James—father of Judas,
one of the 12 disciples,
not the Judas who betrayed Jesus

Jude

Contender for the Faith

Jude, a bondservant of Jesus Christ,
and brother of James...
JUDE 1

Most notable quality: Fearless discernment
Most notable accomplishment: Warning believers of the
coming apostasy
Date lived: Middle of the first century
Name: from "Judah" in Hebrew and "Judas" in Greek
Major text: Jude

Bare Bones Background

As the early church developed and grew, its historical situation
changed. Toward the end of the first century, Christianity had spread
to all levels of society and to every corner of the Roman Empire. The
dangers now facing the church are not of an external nature, even
though there still is extensive persecution. The real threat will come
from within as false doctrines and pagan thought begin to creep into the
churches. With these threats looming over the churches, leaders such
as Jude become compelled to confront these dangers in a short letter
of warning to the churches.

A Quick Sketch

Judas or Jude is the youngest son of Mary and Joseph and the brother of James and the half-brother of Jesus (Matthew 13:55). He and his family live in the northern region of Palestine near the Sea of Galilee. Neither Jude nor his older brothers believe that Jesus is the Messiah during Jesus' ministry years. It isn't until after the resurrection of Jesus that Jude and his brothers believe in Jesus as the Messiah. Jude and his brothers are part of the meetings in the upper room after their Lord's ascension. Jude becomes a radical spokesman for the kingdom of God, and by the time he writes his letter, all the apostles, except John, have been martyred. The church is under political and spiritual attack. Even though Christianity has spread throughout the empire, its spiritual purity is in great jeopardy. Jude calls the church to fight for the truth in the midst of a great spiritual battle. There is no further mention of Jude in Scripture, and there is little if any historical data as to the date of his death.

The Big Picture

▶ **Jude's purpose for writing**—*Jude 1-4*

Jude is about to write a treatise on the salvation that is shared in common by all his readers, but something has caused him to change his topic. False teachers have invaded the churches, denying Christ and using the grace of God to justify their immoral behavior. Jude must warn his readers of this very present danger.

▶ **Jude's warning**—*Jude 5-16*

Jude begins by giving a biblical history lesson of those who were judged for their godless behavior: rebellious Israelites who died in the wilderness because of their unbelief; fallen angels who cohabited with women before the flood; and men who exhibited homosexual behavior and were destroyed in the destruction of Sodom and Gomorrah.

Jude then gives a description of false teachers. They are ruled by their flesh, reject authority, scoff at angelic beings, and mock the things they do not understand. Jude compares false teachers to three spiritually rebellious men in the Bible—Cain (from Genesis), and Korah and Balaam (from Numbers)—and says their evil can be likened to hidden reefs, rainless clouds, uprooted trees, wild waves, and wandering stars.

▶ Jude's exhortation—*Jude 17-23*

Having described the behavior of false teachers, Jude now reminds his readers that Jesus' apostles had warned of this coming defection from the truth. He exhorts them to protect themselves by growing in their understanding of their faith, by praying for the Holy Spirit's guidance, and by looking for Christ's second coming. In the process of fighting for God's truth, they are to show compassion to those who deserve it, and if necessary, to pull others out of the fires of judgment, all the while fearing for their own personal contamination.

▶ Jude's reassurance—*Jude 24-25*

Jude returns to the theme of salvation that he mentioned in the beginning of his letter. He closes his letter with words that will bolster the courage of his readers. Namely, the power of Christ is able to preserve His followers from being overpowered by the enemy.

The Portrait

Jude, like his brother James, humbly identified himself in his letter as a "bondservant of Jesus Christ." To help his readers identify him, Jude also described himself as "the brother of James" (verse 1), who was known and respected by the entire Christian community. Little is known of Jude except what can be drawn from his letter. He wrote with Old Testament prophetic boldness as he spoke for God. Jude called God's people back from false teachings to the truths of the changeless God, who will lead them to victory in the end.

Life Lessons from Jude

Defending your faith is not optional—Jude was concerned that his readers had allowed false teachers to creep into their churches unnoticed. Or, if these teachers had been noticed, his readers had not bothered to confront their error. Jude exhorted his readers to take a stand and "to contend earnestly for the faith" (verse 3). Jude's message is just as relevant today. You cannot afford to stand on the sidelines while others teach falsehoods and slander your Lord or His people. Determine to gain a better understanding of your Bible so that you can stand strong in the defense of God's truth.

Know the value of God's Word—Jude warns against turning away from Christ. He reminds you and me to be careful not to drift away from a faithful commitment to Christ. The remedy for this warning is to value God's Word, which is life and light to the believer. The wisdom found in your Bible is to be desired more that gold. If you know and treasure the truths found in the Bible, you won't be as susceptible to false teachers and their lies about God, about His standards for you, and about your responsibility to be obedient to Him.

Show compassion to the lost—Jude was hard hitting in his call to contend for the faith and resist false teachers. But he also exhorted his readers to show compassion. Many people are just victims of the enemy. From Jude we learn we should use discernment as we witness to three different groups of people: We are to witness with compassion to those who are sincere doubters. To others we are to witness as if we are snatching them from the eternal fire of judgment. And then there are others to whom we need to show mercy, but we also need to exercise caution lest we become contaminated by their sin.

Other New Testament Men Named Judas

Judas the Galilean—He fomented a rebellion against Rome (Acts 5:37).

Judas son of James—He was one of the twelve apostles (Acts 1:13), also called Thaddaeus (Mark 3:18), and Lebbaeus (Matthew 10:3).

Judas Iscariot—He betrayed Jesus for 30 pieces of silver (Matthew 26:14).

Judas of Damascus—He opened his house to Paul after Paul was temporarily blinded while on the road leading into town (Acts 9:11).

Judas Barsabbas—A representative of the Jerusalem church, he was sent back with Paul to Antioch after the Jerusalem counsel (Acts 15:22).

Jesus' Early Years

The Promised One

But when the fullness of the time had come, God
sent forth His Son, born of a woman, born under
the law, to redeem those who were under the law,
that we might receive the adoption as sons.
GALATIANS 4:4-5

&

Most notable quality: The God-Man
Most notable accomplishment: Came to earth to redeem
fallen man
Date: 6 or 5 B.C. to A.D. 26—His birth to public ministry
Name: *Jesus*, meaning "Yahweh is salvation"
Major texts: The four Gospels

Bare Bones Background

From the beginning of biblical history God had promised a Savior
for fallen man (Genesis 3:15). Abraham's descendants were the race
through which this Savior was to come. For centuries, devout Jews all
over the inhabited world regularly searched the Old Testament prophecies in the hopes of understanding when and where this Savior, their
Messiah, would appear.

In the "fullness of the time," God's time, a star appears in the sky.
Wise men from the East, Persia, recognize this bright star as the fulfillment of a prophecy: "A Star shall come out of Jacob; a Scepter shall rise
out of Israel" (Numbers 24:17), and begin the long journey to find this

predicted King. The appearance of this star and the birth of God's Son, the Lord Jesus, is the culmination of thousands of years of anticipation. Jesus is the fulfillment of the covenant promises that were made to Israel that shape the structure of the Old Testament. From this point on, history will revolve around the brief years that Jesus Christ lives on this earth.

A Quick Sketch

It is impossible to treat Jesus as merely another man of the Bible. Jesus is unique. John's Gospel opens by introducing Jesus as the "Word" who existed with God and as God from all eternity. John says that this unique Person became flesh, as the Lord Jesus Christ, and lived among men. John can verify this because he was an eyewitness: "We beheld His glory, the glory as of the only begotten of the Father, full of grace and truth" (John 1:14).

Jesus' brief 33 years of life and ministry compose nearly half of the entire New Testament. And much more could have been written, as John states at the conclusion of his Gospel: "There are also many other things that Jesus did, which if they were written one by one, I suppose, that even the world itself could not contain the books that would be written" (John 21:25).

The Big Picture

▶ **Jesus' birth and infancy**—*Matthew 1:18–2:23; Luke 2:1-39*

It has been 400 years since God last communicated with man. The silence is broken when the angel Gabriel addresses a priest named Zacharias with the news that he and his wife, Elizabeth, are going to have a son, John, who will be a herald for the coming Messiah. The next angelic visitation is to a young Jewish maiden named Mary. She too will have a child, but because she is still a virgin, the conception will take place by supernatural means—the Holy Spirit will come upon her (Luke 1:35).

After receiving assurance of Mary's purity from God in a dream, Joseph, who is engaged to Mary, takes her as his wife and does not have marital relations with her until after Jesus is born. While they await Jesus' birth, they travel to Bethlehem, the tribal home of both, to take part in a worldwide Roman census. It is in Bethlehem that Jesus, the King, is born—not in a palace, but in a stable.

Immediately after Jesus' birth, shepherds arrive with news that they had just been visited by angelic beings announcing the birth of this baby. Eight days later, Joseph and Mary present Jesus, as a firstborn male, at the temple in Jerusalem, which is a few miles from Bethlehem. Joseph and Mary are then amazed by the Holy Spirit's predictions about Jesus, which they hear from a devout man named Simeon, and then they are blessed as they hear from a prophetess named Anna.

Joseph and Mary then travel to Nazareth to get as many of their belongings as they can carry, then return to Bethlehem. When the wise men—the Magi—arrive, Joseph, Mary, and the baby are settled in a home in Bethlehem. As much as two years have elapsed since Jesus' birth. We know this because, when the wise men tell King Herod why they have come, Herod, feeling that Jesus is a threat, orders for all male children two years and under to be killed in the area around Bethlehem. Because of Herod's plot to kill Jesus, Joseph receives a warning from God to flee to Egypt, where the family waits until Herod's death, at which time God instructs them to return to Israel. They intend to return to Bethlehem, but fearing Herod's son, Archelaus, they move back to Nazareth.

▶ **Jesus' life as a child**—*Luke 2:40-52*

Nothing in Scripture indicates that Jesus performed any miracles during his boyhood. In fact, only one significant event is mentioned from this period of Jesus' life. When He reached the age of 12, He traveled with Joseph and Mary to Jerusalem for the annual Passover festival. Mistakenly, He is left behind. They return and search for Him for three days. Finally, they find Him at the temple with the religious scholars, listening and asking questions. This event reveals three things about Jesus at this age:

- He is intensely interested in Scripture (2:46).

- He is aware of His special relationship to His heavenly Father (2:49).

- He is willing to return to Nazareth and be subject to His parents (2:51).

Luke concludes by giving a progress report of Jesus' growth and development until His public ministry begins: "Jesus increased in wisdom and stature, and in favor with God and men" (Luke 2:52).

▶ Jesus' family life and education

After Jesus' birth, Mary and Joseph have four boys (James, Joses, Simon, and Judas), and at least two daughters of their own. Most all the residents of Nazareth are poor, and their homes are small. Jesus' family probably all eat and sleep in one main room. Joseph is never mentioned after Jesus begins His public ministry, which may indicate that Joseph had died. In this case Jesus, as the eldest son, would be responsible for His mother and His brothers and sisters.

All Jewish boys received instruction from their parents and at a local school, usually at a place called a synagogue, after the age of five. Jesus, like the other boys, would attend this formal training before 10:00 A.M. and after 3:00 P.M., being taught to read and memorize Scripture. In between these sessions He would learn his father's trade, carpentry. The scholars in Jerusalem probably would not have been surprised about Jesus' knowledge of Scripture, for all boys of his age memorized Scripture. It would have been His ability to interpret Scripture and relate and apply one passage to another that would set Him apart, as when he listened and asked questions of the teachers at the temple.

▶ Jesus' occupation—carpenter

The ideal in Judaism is that every man have a trade at which to work and that he also be a student of Scripture. Jesus, like most all Jewish boys, became an apprentice of His adopted father, Joseph. Later He would be referred to as both the "carpenter's son" (Matthew 13:55) and as "the carpenter" (Mark 6:3). Jesus would apply Himself to this trade and support His mother and siblings until the beginning of His formal ministry.

Life Lessons from Jesus

God's timetable is perfect. Jesus' arrival on earth was strategically timed. Both the written and vocal message of the resurrection of the Messiah would be understood everywhere in the empire because the Greek language was known and used by the vast majority of people. Politically, Roman rule might have made it safe for Jesus' disciples to travel to other places with a good measure of safety. God's timing is always perfect, even today. God has a plan for your life, but you must do your part in understanding that plan. What can you do? Read His Word. Pray for His wisdom. Seek advice from wise counselors. God has a plan—are you ready to receive and fulfill it?

Jesus submitted to authority. Luke gives great insight into the early years of Jesus in his account about what happened at the Temple. Jesus was a boy who dazzled the religious scholars, but who also willingly went back to His village home and was "subject to" his parents (Luke 2:51). Follow Jesus' example and joyfully submit to those who have authority over you—whether it's your boss at work, the leaders at your church, or your Christian friends (Ephesians 5:21). God will be honored, and you will be blessed.

Humility is a central element of the Christian faith. Can you imagine the God of the universe condescending to come to earth and taking on humanity in order to fulfill His plan for the salvation of sinful man? Paul said Jesus was "in the form of God...[and] made Himself of no reputation, taking the form of a bondservant, and coming in the likeness of men" (Philippians 2:6-7). Humility of heart and mind are crucial in a follower of Christ. You must be humble before you can have a life of useful service for your Master, the Lord Jesus.

An Old Testament Prophecy of Jesus
(700 years before His birth)

For unto us a Child is born, unto us a Son is given;

And the government will be upon His shoulders.

And His name will be called

Wonderful, Counselor, Mighty God,

Everlasting Father, Prince of Peace.

Of the increase of His government and peace there will be no end,

upon the throne of David and over His kingdom,

to order it and establish it with judgment and justice

from that time forward, even forever.

Isaiah 9:6-7

Jesus' Later Years

The Pre-eminent One

The Son of Man has come to seek
and to save that which was lost.
LUKE 19:10

❧

Most notable quality: A teacher with authority
Most notable accomplishment: Died for sinners
Date: Late A.D. 26 to Passover of A.D. 30 (the public ministry of Jesus)
Major text: The four Gospels

Bare Bones Background

In first-century Judaism, discipleship is the normal path to spiritual leadership. Those who desired to become teachers of the law (rabbis) would attach themselves to recognized religious authorities. The training period could take years to complete, by which time the student would be like his teacher (Luke 6:40). Following this pattern, as Jesus taught and ministered, He chose 12 men to be His disciples.

In spite of the wisdom of His teaching and His miracles of healing, Jesus is repeatedly criticized and dismissed by the religious community for not having any formal training under a recognized teacher. The common people, however, quickly realized Him as a gifted teacher who possessed great authority, and they gather in great numbers to hear Him teach.

A Quick Sketch

For some three years, Jesus travels back and forth, mainly throughout the small territories of Galilee, His home area, and Judea, the center of Jewish religion, healing, and teaching. For someone who has had the greatest impact of any man who ever lived, Jesus' travels are very limited. Galilee is 44 miles long and 25 miles wide, while Judea is even smaller.

How did Jesus have such a great impact on the globe when He lived and taught in one small area of the world? Jesus' disciples are the reason, with their empowerment by God's Spirit. Jesus takes a band of 12 ordinary men and, in three years, trains them into a force that shakes the very foundations of the world as they later take the message of Jesus' resurrection and His offer of forgiveness of sin to the ends of the earth.

The Big Picture

▶ **Jesus' baptism**—*Matthew 3:13-17*

By accepting baptism at the hands of John the Baptist, Jesus validates the work of His forerunner and receives an anointing by the Father, as approval, for His own ministry (verse 17). His baptism is an act of consecration to His redemptive ministry. From this time forward the power of the Spirit is upon Him for the fulfillment of His mighty purpose. In addition, by willingly taking part in this rite, which ordinarily is observed by sinners, He identifies Himself with sinners as their sin-bearer (verse 15).

▶ **Jesus' temptation**—*Matthew 4:1-11*

Jesus' baptism can be viewed as marking the beginning of His ministry, and what takes place next helps verify His credentials as the sin-bearer for man. By the power and leading of the Spirit, Jesus is led into the wilderness to be put to the test. At the end of 40 days of fasting, when Jesus is most vulnerable, the devil makes a threefold attempt to persuade Jesus to act on His own, independent of God. (This threefold test was the same ploy used by the devil with Eve in the Garden of Eden: physical appetite, personal gain, and power.) By turning back the adversary each time with scripture, Jesus receives assurance of victory.

▶ Jesus' strategy—*Matthew 10:1-26*

After Jesus' baptism and temptation in the Judean wilderness, He stays nearby, preaching and teaching. During these days in Judea, certain Galileans who have been followers of John show an interest in Jesus, but none will receive a call to follow Jesus until Jesus moves His headquarters to Galilee. When Jesus hears about the arrest of John the Baptist, He moves to the north and spends much of the rest of His ministry in and around Galilee.

It may appear that Jesus' main goal is evangelism, urging people to respond to their King and His coming kingdom. This is a key element of His ministry, but it isn't His main goal. His strategy is to train up disciples who will reach the world with His message. He isn't interested in crowds; He is interested in a few people—specifically, the 12 men He calls to be with Him for the remainder of His ministry. From this time forward until His crucifixion, Jesus will spend more and more time with these men, preparing them to carry on after His return to heaven.

▶ Jesus' crucifixion—*John 13–19*

With mounting opposition from the religious leaders and rejection from the people, Jesus makes His way to Jerusalem for His last Passover on earth, and His sacrificial and brutal death on a cross for the sins of man. Jesus spends his last hours before His betrayal in an upper room with His disciples, including Judas, His betrayer. After Judas leaves to bring the mob, Jesus speaks to His remaining disciples with great compassion and love, warning them of the world's hatred of them. He encourages them to bear a faithful witness of Him as the Spirit enables them.

In one last great prayer, Jesus prays for the protection of the disciples and for their unity, which will insure that the world recognizes His impact on them (John 17). They all leave the upper room and, while in the Garden of Gethsemane, Jesus is arrested. Jesus goes to be tried by both Jewish and Roman authorities, with the verdict already pronounced. All but one of the disciples scatter, leaving three women—Mary, Jesus' mother, Mary, Jesus' aunt, and Mary Magdalene. John, the disciple whom Jesus loved, stays and is at the foot of the cross to be with Jesus until His death.

▶ Jesus' resurrection—*Luke 24:1-51*

Months before His death, Jesus had predicted, in the hearing of His disciples, not only His death but His resurrection three days later (Mark 8:31). Just as He said would be the case, He is executed on a Friday and on Sunday comes the report to the disciples that the tomb is empty. Even the disciples could hardly believe it, but when the Savior appears and explains what has happened, they are overjoyed (Luke 24:44-47). Jesus appears to various people and groups for the next 40 days—then in a final appearance, He ascends into glory (verse 51).

The Portrait

History has affirmed the effects of the life and ministry of the lowly carpenter from Galilee. He is singularly unique of all men who have ever lived. He is a man and shares what belongs to man, apart from sin, yet His existence is from everlasting. His actions and emotions are human, yet His responses are divine. He manifests the kind of life God intends for all men and women. The resurrection and ascension are God's means of recognizing the perfection of His life and ministry. Jesus proclaimed that He is God's only Son, equal with the Father, the Creator of the World, the culmination of history, the Friend of sinners, the Searcher of hearts, the Savior and Judge of mankind. At some point in the future, every knee will bow and every tongue will confess that Jesus Christ is Lord (Philippians 2:11).

Life Lessons from Jesus

Greatness comes from serving others. Jesus came to this earth not to be served but to serve. Following His example, you should be willing to serve others. Even when it comes to leadership, Jesus said being a servant is what qualifies you for a position of authority. Real greatness in Christ's kingdom is shown by service and sacrifice, not ambition or love of power. The way up is down.

There are no shortcuts to spiritual maturity. Even though Jesus was fully God, He was also fully human and grew up in the same way as other humans. He did not bypass one stage of life to get to the next. He did not isolate Himself from the pressures and temptations of life. Jesus' life reminds you that there are no shortcuts for you, either. Maturity and service come with a price you must pay. The price is obedience to God at every step of the way. Pay the price, and you will reap the benefits of a fruitful ministry.

Believing is seeing. Jesus carefully instructed His disciples about how to continue on after His death, yet they didn't believe the initial reports of His resurrection. Thomas is especially known for his disbelief. It took a physical appearance from Jesus for Thomas to believe. May you not be like Thomas, demanding some sort of proof before you act in belief. The disciples believed as eyewitnesses, and you have the opportunity to believe with the eyes of faith, all that the Bible says about Jesus and your eternal destiny. Believe, that you may see.

Declarations That Jesus Is God

Equality with God—"God was His Father, making Himself equal with God" (John 5:18).

Deity—"Are you the Christ, the Son of the Blessed?" Jesus said, 'I am'" (Mark 14:61-62; see also John 9:35-37; 10:38).

The preexistent "I Am" (Yahweh) of the Old Testament— "Before Abraham was, I AM" (John 8:58).

A preexistent member of the Godhead—"Father, glorify Me together with Yourself, with the glory which I had with You before the world was" (John 17:5).

Oneness with God the Father—"He who has seen Me has seen the Father" (John 14:9).

Eternal presence—"I am with you always, even to the end of the age" (Matthew 28:20).

Other Books by Jim George

BARE BONES BIBLE® HANDBOOK
The perfect resource for a fast and friendly overview of every book of the Bible. Excellent for anyone who wants to know more about the Bible and get more from their interaction with God's Word.

A MAN AFTER GOD'S OWN HEART
Many Christian men want to be men after God's own heart...but how do they do this? George shows that a heartfelt desire to practice God's priorities is all that's needed. God's grace does the rest.

A HUSBAND AFTER GOD'S OWN HEART
Husbands will find their marriages growing richer and deeper as they pursue God and discover 12 areas in which they can make a real difference in their relationship with their wife.

A YOUNG MAN AFTER GOD'S OWN HEART
Pursuing God really *is* an adventure—a lot like climbing a mountain. There are all kinds of challenges on the way up, but the awesome view at the top is well worth the trip. This book helps young men to experience the thrill of knowing real success in life—the kind that counts with God.

GOD'S MAN OF INFLUENCE
How can a man have a lasting impact? Here are the secrets to having a positive and meaningful influence in the lives of everyone a man meets, including his own wife and children.

GOD LOVES HIS PRECIOUS CHILDREN
(coauthored with Elizabeth George)

Jim and Elizabeth George share the comfort and assurance of Psalm 23 with young children. Engaging watercolor scenes by artist Judy Luenebrink and delightful rhymes by Jim and Elizabeth bring the truths of each verse to life.

GOD'S WISDOM FOR LITTLE BOYS
(coauthored with Elizabeth George)

The wonderful teachings of Proverbs come to life for boys. Memorable rhymes play alongside colorful paintings for a charming presentation of truths to live by.